PUT IT ON PAPER

"ALL YOUR THOUGHTS AND FEELINGS"

DeVondia R. Roseborough

PUT IT ON PAPER

Published By: DeVondia R. Roseborough

Copyright © 2005 by DeVondia R. Roseborough

Cover Design By: Moye' www.moyephoto.net

Stylist: LaToya Adams

Cover Model: DeVondia R. Roseborough, Make-Up P.K Designs

ISBN-978-0-6151-9523-0

To order additional copies of Put It On Paper or to contact the author visit: www.rasberrirose.org

Printed in the United States of America

I dedicate this book to all the women and men, who have put themselves and others at risk, use this as a lesson learned not worth repeating. Follow your dreams and do not sacrifice your mind, body and soul for the sake of love.

DeVondia Roseborough

Author with a Purpose

"A person will take you as far as YOU allow them to."

Acknowledgments

Throughout this long and worthy process, many people went through the storm with me, enjoyed the sun when my medications would not allow me, and exhaled for me when I did not want to take another breath. I appreciate every one of you for your given season for your reasons in my life; for friendship, wisdom, patience with me talking about a book (Put it on Paper) for 6 years and for unconditional love and respect.

Though I walked through the shadow of death, I continue not to fear evil. Therefore, haters I rebuke you in the precious name of Jesus and pray daily for protection against you. My Lord, my Savior all honor and the highest praise for what you have done in my life.

To my beautiful daughters, Pearl & Pumpkin, I love you and I thank you for putting up with mommy while I put it on paper. To my Mother, woman you have been an inspiration to me through it all and I thank you for the tough love and being the best mom any girl could ever hope to have. My best girls in the world, Wanda Hughes-Glenn, Tiffany Barringer, Melissa Gibson, LaToya Adams, Angela Bush-Robinson, Michelle Brooks, and Rhonda Miller; Thank you ladies so much you all are so special to me and a special thump in this chest beats for you all. You all held me down when I wanted to let go. Popee my Stepfather, Thanks for stepping in and being the man we all needed in our lives. My lovely sister Lateka, (Mini Me) I am so glad we finally got it together, I love you and my nephew Dillion so very much. I appreciate you helping me out when I could not help myself.

Candy, Candy Candy, My cousin Noteka Kenyatta Walker, I told you I had you girl! I am proud of you for the many accomplishments and breakthroughs you overcame. Raising Shaquanda, school, and work...you took after me! I love you cuzzo. My Big Uncle, Shaky Redd I love you! My crazy brother Terry Gerome Cunningham, I love you big brother I am going to build you a house in the back yard. SMILE! To my loving Godchildren; the daughters, Shaquavia Bush; I love you sweetheart, stay close and bloom into the elegance of tomorrow's woman. Shamia Glenn, Hey round brown, keep dancing lady bug, Laporsha Barringer, DJ Smooth, I got to get you that DJ equipment; Shanice Barringer, with your smart behind...keep reading lady. The sons, Marcellus Marcez, Robert Devon, Manasseh Withers Kasy Teran, Ashvin Tyler, Christian Jahon; your God mama loves you all, become the men that God says in His word for you to be. Men of Valor filled with the Holy Spirit and respect for self and others.

My Sisters Nita, Edwina, Brother Michael I love you all too. We need to get close and stay close. Hey Nephew Daveion and Vaderian and to all my nephews and nieces I do not know, Auntie loves you. My Father, Gerome Roseborough, I love you. My Aunt Geneva Hood Hudson, Mary Frazier, My Great-Aunts Beufort Wilson and Bea-trice Massey; St Mark 16:18 "They shall lay hands on the sick, and they shall recover." I love you all so very much.

To my cousin Ebony Henderson (Skeeter) I told you Shrek was coming out with a part 3. I love you and the family so much. To my dear Cousin Tumina Walls-Parker (Myron) Isaiah & Kaleb; you all are special to me; you have been there for the announcement of the test, through the storm of the test and look at the outcome. You believed in me and I love you for your faithfulness. Sherika Lawhorn (Amari) I love you Lil sis, Keep doing you, but keep God first, cause without Him all else fails.

I must close it out now but not before, I shout out a few more people for their love and support; Cheryl Mayfield-Brown, Andrea Blackstone, Marcus Massey, Katina Ammons, Moye' (Book Cover Designer), Michelle Dorsey (The woman with the rubber hammer), Ronnie, Rob and Roderick Burris and Cousin Poo Poo; Aunt Judy (Chip), Michael 'Hulkabuck' Brown I love you all! Dashoppe Barber Shop; Rob T. & Markie Thanks for the support;

MasterKuts Barber & Beauty Salon: JR, Slow, Big Game, Ms. Doris, Big John, Jerry, Toya (Rip) and Barbara (Throne); Thanks for allowing me to share my story and draw needed awareness on the subject of HIV/AIDS in your shops. Tomekia Erwin & family, Lashawn Weddington-Spears & family, Aunt Sonia and Ms. Valerie & family; you all mean the world to me. To the gorgeous one, you know who you are, thanks for the time you spend and the memories we share. The hottest station in the Carolina's WPEG Power 98 No Limit Larry, Tone-X, Church Boy, Janine Davis, and the promotions team for supporting me on the college tours. All churches, schools, especially West Charlotte High School; Ms. Pace English III class, community events, sororities, public health departments, workshop providers, conferences that have allowed me to do what God left me here to do.

Thanks to you all. Gayle Scott, Martha Huxster, Pansy Borden, Glenda Horton-Manning, Tammy Jones, Jerome Moore, Kwain Bryant, Thomas Barksdale, Cheris Hodges, Stan Warring, Pastor WJ & First Lady Ruby Neal; My care Team, Dr. Jessica Saxe, Dr. David Wenrib, Dr. Thomas Verville, Metrolina AIDS Project, and RAIN (Regional AIDS Interfaith Network). Last but certainly not least my church family at New Covenant Bibleway Church,

Bishop C.M. Beatty and First Lady Deborah Beatty, I love every one of you, Thanks for the love, prayers and continued support.

ACCESS GRANTED

"You have so much to talk about, Jermaine said. You ought to write a book. Put it on Paper all your thoughts and feelings. You have a story to tell." I thought about what Jermaine said to me. Everything that he says puts me on my toes. He inspires me to think out side the box and be creative with my thoughts and feelings. October 2001, I attended the Johnson C. Smith Homecoming Parade in Charlotte, NC. I spotted the WPEG Power 98 FM promotions van with co-host, No Limit Larry of the Breakfast Brothas Morning Show. {Now No Limit Larry and the Morning Maddhouse}, I shouted to No Limit that I had my Power 98 gold card, which if you have your card when asked by a WPEG Power 98 FM personality you could win a prize. He told me to come to the van to see what he had. He passed me a 5x7 notebook with Jay Z on the front and back promoting his Blueprint album.

After the parade I came home poured me a nice glass of Chardonnay, turned on the Mary J. and started the manuscript you are about to read. I put the book down after writing in it for over a year and a half. Not knowing what the end was going to be. So now, you begin the drama in my life that unfolds gritty issues that created the rose that continues to grow with no weeds attached.

THE PAST

I have come to believe that a person is angry for a reason. No matter what the problem is discrimination, drug abuse, sexual assault/rape the problem stems from somewhere and most likely someone. I had reasons for my nasty attitude, not to say it justified me being an obnoxious person, but it acknowledged that it was a problem within me crying out for help. Please know that it was hard for me to get to this point of expressing the situations that you are about to read. Some of the content may be offensive and hard for many of you to read and some may wonder why I am putting my business out for every one to know, just know that I have to take you were I have been to get you to why I stand. Through my faith and forgiving heart I forgave those that abused me, the hardest part was forgiving me. Taking my emotions out on family and friends was how I dealt with the anger I carried inside. I realized that when I thought I had actually finished my book that it was not complete. There was more to the story than I was willing and ready to tell. I continue to heal even as I type this it lets me know that I am growing, maturing, loving, accepting of my past, and geared up for what the future holds. The piece that you are about to read is my actual beginning. I was a little girl standing out in front of my duplex on Dundeen Street bouncing a plastic purple and white ball that had a cloud like pattern. A man pulled up in front of my home in a long gray car and asked me where Dundeen Court was. I hesitated as I took small steps towards the car. I knew about stranger danger, so I froze in my last step and pointed down the street towards the dead end circle called Dundeen Court. When I looked up he had his penis in his hand stroking it up and down with an evil smirk upon his face. Luckily, for me he drove off. Was I lucky? I picked my ball up and bounced it with a continuous thrust, trying to block what I had seen out of my mind. I did not tell anybody. I was five or six years old. She placed her hands on my shoulders and directed me towards the bathroom. The house was clear of every one that would have noticed why we were going in there together. The body of the white porcelain tub was wide with an enormous belly. The tiny sized bathroom accommodated with the necessities for bathing and eliminating waste. She placed a white towel down on the floor in front of the tub and told me to take off my clothes. The four rounded corners had scalloped embroidered legs with cobwebs on the right leg of the tub. Silence was among us as she took off her clothes. She told me to lie down on my stomach, I lay fearful and unsure of what was about to take place. Her large brown body stood over me as I wondered why I am here. She lay on top of me and rotated her large frame on my buttocks. I wondered what she was doing as secretion moistened my tender backside. As she reached her climax, she shivered and shook. I had no feeling to what had transpired, just what was she doing. It must have felt good, because it happened repeatedly. She said get up as she reached for the bath cloth and soap and wiped my lower bottom area down, which was drenched with her bodily fluids. "You better not tell anybody!" she said, and I did not. I cry every time I watch Antoine Fisher I was in the third grade. He pulled out his penis and told me, "You have never seen a dick this big before." He would get between my legs and roll on me after he pretended to play fight with me. Seducing me with words as his body wiggled a feeling between my legs. Was I a bad kid for feeling this way? I was 11 years old. My mom sent me to neighborhood store on a Saturday evening to get a pair of panty hose for church. I put on my coat and walked to the store with my hands in my coat pocket. As I got to the corner of Caldwell and 9th Street, I stopped for a car. A car filled with Caucasian teenagers yelled out obscenities and spit, no let me rephrase that hawked on my coat and face. I remember my mom being in a rage, out for blood. With tears in her eyes, I scared while my mom said burn that coat. Here I am now with the burden off my shoulders. I speak freely about the factors that lead up to the risky choices that made and make a difference in my life and others. At age 33, the month before my 34th birthday in 2005 I told my mother about the molestations I endured and carried with me through out the years. I explained to her that it was not her fault and I dealt with it. I attended counseling and support group meetings to help me cope. I remember meeting with a group of women and someone had molested each one of them. We released the baggage and anger we suffered by blowing out through our mouths towards a candle that sat in the middle of the circle. As we stood in a circle with our arms wrapped around one another the smell was like no other, not a bad breath smell, but a smell that confirmed it was time to let go of the negativity that suppressed us. We then told to breathe in new air, happy thoughts and faith. As this took place, the air was clean and crisp with nothing to obvious including dust to detour our path to serenity. I had forgiven everyone that caused me to endure the unnatural, but I never forgot. Now it is time for me to reveal the risky behaviors in which a test made a change in my life, so that I can in turn help the many enduring the same issues breakthrough. Unlike what I did, talk to someone, do not carry this burden alone and know that it is not your fault. Tell someone you trust I wish I did. In addition, always keep the faith.

THE BEGINNING

The time is now that my life is as sweet as it is. My Cadillac caught an attitude and cost me some change. Leroy the mechanic is looking out for the pocketbook. Interesting to say Jermaine, the tire guy at the auto shop brings sunshine to my life every time I see him. Sexy, honey caramel coated skin with deep dark eyes sheltered by thick black hair to protect his eyes from harm. Jermaine is not your typical male. Before I get to my ending, I need you to understand my beginning. At this point in my life for the very first time my history of scandalous, heartbreaking, yet courageous relationships has ever, ever, ever, ever had a man so passionate, so caring, intellectually inclined, diverse, skeptical of many things, and willing to endure the challenge. A marvelous sophisticated man I had not met before in my life. I can go on but you know how some people do when you hear of a good catch. Jermaine is the man you want to take home to meet your mama, grandma and dad will even like him. Why, well mainly because we are so compatible.

He participates in my world and he shares so much love between those he encounters. Not only are we both Libra born but we also share the same likes to the perceptive voice of Mary J. Blige and Friday's Black Bean Soup. We share similar dislikes and he respects my opinions. A keep it real type of person. Damn the brother I want to marry! We both have children and he lives in a small town in South Carolina bordering my city in North Carolina. This Palmetto State native so full of charisma can charm you into unforgettable thoughts. The inspiration for this book came from Jermaine, He told me "Rose you have so much to talk about; you ought to write a book. Put it on paper all your thoughts and feelings, he continued, you have a story to tell." The sex well I guess I will leave that alone. As I said earlier, you know how some of you do. He completes me, he understands me. We share an experience that has prepared us for one another. If a man could be a DIVA, he is the one. He is no Bitch Ass punk or a push over. He is sensitive to my needs and he stands firm for which he believes. A hardworking individual, who is aware of his responsibilities and handles his business, always willing to learn more and the heart to teach, Jermaine, has opened my eyes to a light like no other man has done before. You cannot say that good men are not out there. I just needed patience. I was turning 30 and not looking forward to it.

Wishing the double digit was 19 instead. I claimed to realize that after 18 was 19 and trying to live in that tender, yet vulnerable and inexperienced age. Shit, I became even more relaxed at turning the big 30. In the beginning, God created the heavens and the earth. Despite the tragedy that hit our nation September 2001, my heart was fluttering to a newfound love affair. Determined to keep the fire burning in this relationship I will now take you on a journey of drama. I was ready for what ever came my way.

Take this book to understand what is real, for edutainment or just to add to your bestseller's collection, but for whatever reason take it serious.

For the sake of sued by others, a few names of people, some places and things have been altered!

At the tender age of 17, I was head over heels for anyone who wanted me. I felt I was unattractive. Well I was shit, thick ass glasses, size 26 clothes, a size 10 in shoes and an attitude that would rip a start for a girl fight in a heartbeat. At 19, I met Andrew. He had a girl named Tasha and for a while, I was unaware that there was someone else. The brother had the nerve to tell me that the reason why I could not visit his apartment was that he did not have any furniture. Being embarrassed was what he said to express his reasoning behind the deceit. Liar, liar, liar! Yeah I got up in that apartment, sure did. I ate, shit, slid vaginal juice across the sheets as I got up from the sweat drenching sex we had almost every day. The brother was so damn smart that he would take the sheets off the bed and straight to the washer as he passed me my bra I would try to leave up under a pillow. Yep, sprung, the very first person I was head over heels. He was my first in many sexual escapades and he cared for me, at least I thought. The day the test results read positive to a September 1991 due date for a bouncing baby was not what I needed at this time. In addition, I did not need him asking me "What was I going to do." My heart sunk even lower, believing what my mom use to say all the time, "a hard head will make a soft ass." On February 13 in the year 1991, I had an abortion. I could not take care of myself no less a baby. I could not keep this baby. I asked God to forgive me and protect me against harm. I took a locket that belonged to my deceased grandmother. In the room were the procedure took place, I clutched tightly around the locket and prayed as the noise roared loudly. As I fought the anesthesia to see what I had gotten myself into, I remembered the doctor telling

11

me not to fight it, so I did not. As the nurse so rudely jacked me off the table, slapping a super sized maxi pad between my legs escorting me into the next room to recover from it all. All I could remember was the airplane mobile that hung above the table I laid on spinning round and round. I got home late that day after spending time at my good friend Cassandra's house sleeping the medicine off. I recall my mom talking to my biological father on the phone telling him, "I believe she had an abortion." I did not have the nerve to tell her that I was pregnant. Therefore, I did not say a word. Things could not have gotten better. I got pregnant again, later on that year. A tall dark glass of fine wine my oldest daughter's father was to me and the relationship did not become of what I desired and for respect for him and her I share no details of our relationship with the exception of a beautiful female Leo born. A sweet young thing, having no idea what was going on or how her mom had screwed up time after time. All I knew was I had some growing up to do. The men I have been involved with did not possess a degree, no less a high school equivalent. I was looking for more than taking care of a Negro and kissing his ass every time he bent over. I was sick and tired of the no job holding; do not know how to hold a conversation ass buster. I always knew what I wanted to do. I dreamed a continuous dream of being a famous singer and producer of R&B music. From ghetto queen to Diva Doll, Yeah baby, the big house with a beautiful backyard, a driveway to hold the mint green Q-45 and black Cadillac Escalade. The good life is what I was in search for. God knows I deserved it. However, I had to realize that only I could make it happen. I knew depending on half ass men who didn't care to listen to my thoughts and respect my feelings was not going to help me get ahead. I allowed my pride and lack of self-awareness stripped through re-occurring drama. Like Mary J. says, "No More Drama." I feel you Mary. Renting appliances with high finance charges on cheap ass furniture, rent turned into mortgage, Hyundai payments elevated to a 92 Cadillac Sedan Deville, insurance, food, clothes, entertainment, and get high fair. Yes, I said it. We all have done something we had no business or dare not to share. I smoked blunts like an overheated Suburban on Independence Blvd at 5:20 p.m. on a Friday afternoon in 90 degree heat. Faithfully I smoked before breakfast, lunch, and dinner and in between snacks, before, during and after sex. I had to have it. Dealing with these sorry ass brothers and silly acting females, I concluded that I was better off with a blunt and my JVC pumping the crisp sounds of whatever the mood called for. Puff away the bitches in one pull. If certain females are not smiling in your face pretending to be your friend, they are stabbing you in your back pushing up on your man while holding a cup to borrow some sugar for that red Kool Aid she is about to fuck up. I found I would rather be in the company of the opposite sex than with other females because it was always some shit popping off. Men were my best company with the exception of my usual female entourage. Bump what every one else was thinking. You do not have to have sex with them. The people in the hood are going to determine that for you. At one point, people called me Ms. Parker. Remember Mrs. Parker from Ice Cube's Friday. You named me right Ms. Robin Black. Ms. Parker was always ready with her Diana Ross eyes and exquisite style. She was different from who I really was and needed to be. She had so much wisdom and a sensitive heart that been trampled on. She began using her ability to attract men as her weapon for defeat and to get back at hoe's that got on my nerves. A woman with low self-esteem, street mentality, book smarts and common sense knew what to do to another woman, that bought on the fever or should I say drama. It was not in my nature to call Housing Authority risking your kids having some where to stay or DSS to have your food stamps or AFDC cut off. Trap them off in their heart, their man. Then I met Gary, a soft-spoken person, with no get up and go about him. He was an attractive person, very passive, his dress code sucked, and this joker had

14

the nerve to stay out all night and hang with his friends. The majority of the time I stayed pissed off at his ass. He had the nerve to be sexually active in and out of my family tree and if a job fell in the bed with him, he would jump the hell up and out of that Sealy Posturepedic. I think back on this day with the smooth sounds of Mary J's song telling me "Changes I've been going through." Thinking how I have corrupted my life even more with men not worthy of my time, my heart or my body. This is what I get playing in the devil's playhouse. 1990 and 1991, I had become pregnant 2 times by men that did not share the same feeling for me that I had for them. Two years later I became a mother again to another bouncing baby girl, my chocolate drop, I hid the pregnancy from my family up to the seventh or eighth month. I found out my mother knew all along she saw the prenatal vitamins on my dresser when she visited my apartment one day. I learned through this that experiences could take you farther if you learn to hold on to the why and not the hurt. Analyze it, move on and know better next time. As my Grandmother used to say, "Only a fool will make the same mistake twice." As you read on you will see I was a damn fool. In addition, you cannot hide anything from your mother. I know I have done things to entice men, of course, who has not? Even though my size 14 body can stand some sit-ups, push-ups and a personal trainer I am a beautiful woman. I started to see the beautiful eyes my friends told me I had hidden behind my glasses. Especially an ex-boyfriend of mine, we went to the lake one evening to walk and talk about our relationship, he stopped and grazed my arms with his fingertips causing goose bumps to invade my skin. He took my glasses off and expressed to me how beautiful my eyes were and that I should not hide them behind the glasses. Not wanting to loose him, I squinted to see for months. Like the great Michael Jackson song PYT, Pretty Young Thing. At this point of my life, I started to like myself, only because someone else did. I started to shed the pounds by walking and drinking more water and of course cutting back on the fried chicken wings with ranch dressing. I did not think about why someone else did not see what I saw in me and if I did, I used it to my advantage. As I began to love myself, I appreciated me more and more. Shit it did not matter because I fucked up again.

TRYING TO PUT IT TOGETHER

"I'll be back," is what he had said, knowing I will not see him until tomorrow, or maybe not at all. Listening to them complain about nothing worth hearing, not have a job, mess around on you and burn you with a nasty ass disease, that's curable of course. Not my Boo, he is different; he keeps it real with me. He is sincere about his business, and when he expresses himself, the energy of his conversations is breath taking, boy I could go on, but as I said before, you know how some of you do. I take everything serious when it comes down to him. Hoping and praying that this beautiful beginning will have a beautiful end. I have always been the type to loving-to-love and hating- to-hurt. I gave my all and it meant so much to me to love. I know you have had a man who needed commissary or maybe not. Ms. BellSouth wanted her palms greased with coins on time, and if it were not she would slap a block on the line with no permission. It was by choice to send $30.00 here $15.00 there. Shit, I was not rich. I had things to do and he could not do it locked down. Writing all the letters, the numerous visits, and reading all of his was not the type of relationship I envisioned. I decided to go back to college, I helped build my home 6 years ago and I can say I am truly blessed. During the tough times my best friend Wanda would say, "DeVondia things will get better, you will see." I waited, waited, and waited, until Jermaine blew in with the wind that swept me off my feet. I started attending a nice little church in the hood. I learned a lot on how to accept the blessings when they came not when I asked for them. The Federal Agents met my Boo Bear at his State of North Carolina appointed court date I lost an investment of $3000.00 or more and my car to the repossession man. Shit, I did not want a Hyundai anyway. Nevertheless, I gained patience, freed my attitude of negativity and was ready to conquer the world for the very first time ever in my life. Yeah right. I know I was here for a reason and always feeling dangerous towards others including myself was not in the plan. I was a walking time bomb ready to explode. The only thing that relaxed my mind, body and challenged me to do I do not know what was that sticky icky icky, a blunt of that fire. Shit I am shell now feeling so fresh and so clean. Everything seemed so clear to me nothing else beside my children mattered. I really did care about whom I was and what I needed to do to get ahead. I have the knowledge to make things manifest. In addition, I have been through enough anger management workshops and interpersonal relationship series to instruct classes and paid for it. I learned more about how others perceived me through actions of my own. I believe Jermaine took the same classes, just kidding. I say this because this nickel slick brother was always trying to get in my head. "So why didn't you just ask?"

Dear Jermaine,

I have so much to live for and so much more to be thankful. You came into my life and opened up the windows on my dark cloudy sight. You hold me so tight and close leaving me in a vegetable state. Mindless, with no cares because I feel safe in your arms. The feeling is great and I admire your style. Your touches, accompanied by electrifying pulses which tremble my body and leave me helpless like a newborn babe, full of warmth and ecstatic about it all. In disbelief over this wonderful transition my life has made I never thought I would love again.

Yeah, this is what brothers want to hear. That you are on the Y, whooped, lost my damn mind because past relationships caused me to be insecure. I continue with, now I feel free to say its okay. I know no relationship is perfect. There are many disagreements to deal with and many more to count on; however, we as intelligent individuals seek some of the same things. To be loved and to love with integrity, respect, honesty, with a sense of direction filled with pride and joy, faith, determined at making it last, let's not forget about educated, beautiful and the will to challenge and be challenged. I cannot say I will not say things I really do not mean to say, that every night I will cook you a hot meal, that I will drive the truck every day. However, I can say that I will be honest, true to myself first and always to you, to be your one and only, and to live for us nothing especially bullshit matters, only our happiness. Meeting your kids was a treat, planning and partaking in family outings, like beach trips, movies, and concerts, loving one another and bonding as a family.

Love,

Rasberrirose

PS   Acceptance is pure when it comes to being honest about how you truly feel and I felt my prayers answered. All the work you put into keeping me happy helped put a sister on her toes so like a grant I had to match every thing you did and more, for the right reasons of course....

I wrote Jermaine this letter hoping and praying the day, he would read it. Hoping the inspiration he penetrates through me is the same for him. Wake up, it is not a dream you too can one day find your soul mate. We want a mate, whom cook, cleans, will make a mean spaghetti pie and a hell of a love maker. We seek the poetic conversationalist with so much sex appeal. Hey! I have been disappointed to when the real shit hits the fan and all of what he did to get you cease. Nevertheless, the first time I realized anyone can make me laugh, but it takes a hell of a person to make me smile.

MS. ATTITUDE

Always wanting shit her way was how it was. I wanted the cake, pie, Moet, weed, dick, at whatever cost. With nothing but what matters in the world. My thoughts were on getting rich and staying rich. I fucked up more than a few times. Especially when I expressed my dreams to someone I trusted and profits increased for the thief to purchase the bigger house, the blacked out jeep, diamonds on the wrist and…oh! I forgot where I was going with this. Forgive me for my flashback. Well let just say I am still wishing and planning a strategy to conquer Bill Gates. Just remember not to tell all of your dreams to folk; you could risk them claimed by others or worse. Yeah, it is on now. Getting mad was her problem, I say her because she no longer is a part of me. She was evil, vindictive, and conflicts were the highlights of her day. Cursing somebody out, fucking someone's man, boy she was a total Ms. Universe. Who has been there done that. Shit it was time to move on to the next level. Constantly someone or some circumstance blocked me from getting what I strove to get or was it me. I know by now you think I have Bipolar disorder well I do not. I named my different personalities based on how I felt and if you ticked me off, I would forewarn you who was coming out. The one I called Vanessa, boy you did not want to fuck with Vanessa. You did not want to cross her the wrong way especially on a good day. Living that way was not for me I wanted to be born again. A second chance was all I wanted. No cares, no worries, no hurting. My mama used to say, "It will get worse before it gets better." Lord knows she was right. I had to change Vonda. No one wanted to be told off all the time and believe me I hated me too. Do not get it twisted even I wished I were not born and even contemplated suicide. Just thought about it, that is all. I realized that I was hurting myself more than anyone else could, why because I came to realize that I am worthy of being who I am as long as I do not cause harm or threaten the other person involved. My purpose has to fulfill before my last day on this earth. As early as the 4th grade, my teacher at First Ward Elementary, Mrs. G. asked me what I wanted to be when I grew up. My dream for so long had been children wanting and needing to be cherished, honored for their success, respected, and taught how to love themselves first. We as people endure some of the best and worst in our relationships and no matter how bad we feel or how down we become we stick in there. Wake up people, if you do not have the coffee brewing in your maker then smell some body else's. Treat yourself the way you want that mate to treat you. Therefore, when the time comes for you to challenge the harvest moon, you will not settle for less.

GOALS

It is important to put together a plan. If you are in the grocery store high ass hell and you know, as well as I do that once you fall into the Food Lion on Beatties Ford Road you better have a shopping list, or your budget is fucked up. Believe me we have to see the plan on paper before we act on it, or if someone else is already getting it done and you feel you can do a better job, "stop it!" Think for yourself and concentrate on you, Find what it is you want to do, discover what you hope to get out of it, how long will it take? Make your mission as attainable as possible. How will you handle the difficult times? Who will serve as your support team? Believe me you will need positive reinforcement from family and friends to help you make it to the top. Please stay away from toxic people, places, and things. You have to be around positive influential people to help you through the hard times. To keep it on the real, if we stop hating one another we may be okay. Look I said we might, because somebody somewhere is going to twist some new shit in the game and we will be back to square one again. Like the old folks say, "the devil is busy,' put that devil under your feet and handle your business. We cannot let toxic individuals, bad places, and not needed things hinder our paths to success. Be honest with your plan and be realistic with what you say you are going to do. A goal can be hard only if you allow your challenge to challenge you. In order for a person to want you, you must know what you want in you. You are the center of someone's eye and in their eyes you may be a fashion designer, a gourmet cook, a topless dancer, and many other things you would not have dreamed of doing to impress them. What are you doing to attract your mate? Remember you must contain the fire to the same degree or above. What you do to get him/her is what you must do to keep him/her. Do not forget to add some flavor to it. Flash something extra, be creative, be spontaneous and have a good time doing it. Because if the love is real, you and he are satisfied about the relationship you have bloomed to last for eternity. I have always wanted to take a romantic trip with someone all alone, with candles filling the air with the aroma of peaches. The color of red roses beautifying the environment as the fireplace trickles the flames seen on the dual champagne goblets, the soft sounds of Alexander O'Neal and pure ecstasy. The most romantic outing I have experienced was a trip my ex and I took to High Point NC to visit my Aunt Genny and stayed in a stale smelling motel off I-85 N. I wanted something better than that, you know Jacuzzi, roses, wine etc. Yeah I know what you are thinking, that ungrateful bitch. No darlings I deserve better. I treat myself better than that so what I expect from others should be an even swap no swindle. Of course, I have fears; a fear of heights is one. I would love to fight this fear with my new mate by riding a stallion without being afraid and of course falling off. I want the romantic moon lit on the shores of Jamaica. I want the waterfall action from behind the stream of water as my lover caresses me softly. I will endure the obstacle of a first class plane ride overseas to vacation. We all do. Hey, people live and learn some of this shit is not going to happen. Focus on what is realistic. Please do not get caught up, it can be a trap. When doubt is near shit will prevail as you have fucked up again.

TRUST

Why do we hurt so much? We see a fine brother/sister with a glow in his/her eye and wrist and we turn into human cupcakes. Yeah I said it I sure did. We need to be open-minded about the situation, especially when shit isn't going right, and you know deep in your heart he/she is not worthy of you and your time. We try anyway and look like a fool with a set of wet, with somebody's pickle juiced nuts in your mouth and hair in your teeth. Fuck that shit, wine and dine yourself if the motherfucker does not want to. Make your expectations known in the beginning before you make a commitment to Dr. Fuck up, being sure that he/she can reciprocate. If not you will only set yourself up for another disappointing period in your life. I asked God to help me because I did not want to look like a silly sally sausage head. Hell, I do not know about you, but I love me and you should feel the same way about you. You are special so act like it. Remember, "A person will only treat you as far you allow them too."

LYING ASS

I know my girl Sunshine Anderson said it best, "Heard it all before." No one has time for that bullshit. Telling lies is a turn off for me. If you truly want me out of your life then make your nose grow. "I'll be back," "I did it baby," or "I promise" are some lame ass excuses for doing whatever you say you did not do. One fool asked me to fix his favorite meal, Rib eye Steak, Brown Rice, Italian Cut Green Beans and Crescents. I honestly thought the brother was coming home, but my gut begged to differ. You women know about the woman's intuition. He was just placing an order to keep my ass from thinking he was not. I was sick of it and you should be. I am tired of men not keeping it real. I do not mind staying at the crib, I enjoy my home I feel safe in my domain. Therefore, it is not as if I am waiting on a lie to unfold. I have a motto I live by and I need to share it with you. Folks are always doing something to corrupt or try to anyway, your mind and heart. I have always been a firm believer that no one can use me. It is my decision to say yes or no to what ever he or she says to me, whether it is about money, a date, or a favor. From me to you, "A person can take you as far as you allow them." I am a firm, yet nice woman with red devil experience and I do not want to feel taken advantage. I do not want enemies nor do I want or need phony people in my life. I have waited so long to find someone to be honest with him as well as to me. I am not accepting lies, shit I cancelled the episode drama FROM MY LIFE, what about you?

DREAMS

I know you probably set the mood in your head, closed your eyes as he lights the candles and imagine the bearskin rug. Girl umm, the fantasy of every woman probably is fulfilled by her thoughts alone. Hell, I got the best sleep when I strike up my own dream. It is possible; think long enough about how you want it, how it smells, where you want it, and when. Then lay back and let absolutely nothing disturb your groove, your mood, or your concentration. Now if you can make up a high profile life and enjoy simulations of joy with no pain added, then why in the name of Jesus can you not live in the real world the same way? Some dreams have told me what I have felt all along about worthless, jobless, uneducated brothers and some have simply opened my eyes to reality. Wake up people some dreams best left forgotten while others are worth revisiting. Do you remember the dreams when you woke up fear of falling you wake up tears in your eyes and realize you are smack dead in the middle of your bed? You thought that shit only happened to you. Well we all experience something in similar instance that makes us nod yeah, been there done that too. Well, just know we have to wake up sometimes before we realize what is really going on. Think about it.

The one and only, I am Diva doll, Dee Dee, Diva Don Da Da. Known to cuss your ass out, roll my eyes and smoke you under the table. Lately I have been feeling good about life. What is in store for me was the unanswered question. I was ready to explode into orbit and nut on the world. Fuck, you Negroes that talked about me, fuck you Negroes that are still talking about me. I am just keeping it real, "Straight out Da Ville" (What it do Major & Rip). I am a mother, friend, singer, and lover, caring, a dynamic cook, courageous, victorious, intelligent, and levelheaded. I am Vonda. The one who says I have to get it. I am going to have it; I am going to do whatever takes to keep it. Doing the best I know to get ahead. Define who you are and ask yourself are you happy with your discovery? An exercise I like to do with students when conducting self-awareness sessions is to ask my audience to imagine they had a 2 year old daughter, and she goes into your closet and puts on your favorite pair shoes. Would you be pleased with her walking in your footsteps and most importantly would she be proud of you? Now let that marinate for a minute. Moreover, continue reading.

I am whom I am, nurtured by my mother and stepfather and the absence of my father. My parents were divorced when I was young in age. I knew my father and his whereabouts and I figured that was what mattered. I was cared for, nurtured, and scolded. Let me rephrase that I got my ass whooped. Fly swatter, dishcloth, shit mama was and still is the number one stunner. I have a beautiful mother and regret the days I took her granted. I was fortunate to have parents who did not abuse drugs and alcohol. However, I had a great deal of friends who took that route. They used drugs and alcohol to tune out their experiences they endured as a scapegoat for not succeeding in life. My mom is the best mom any girl could wish for with pride and dignity. My Mom has much respect in the community in which she lives and works. My mother is a fighter for what is fair and right, a friend, and an entrepreneur, sassy, classy, stern, loving and spiritually grounded.

I Love You Ma!

HOW CAN YOU SAY THAT?

I have done many things that I am not proud of and feel by standing firm that God will forgive me of my sins past, present, and those that have not been committed. I am not perfect and neither are you, so deal with it. The world does not revolve around your good times or bad times. You do! You might ask how I can categorize myself as a role model and used to smoke pot. I have a story to tell and folks want to hear the truth not bull shit ass lies or somebody else made up drama. This is some real stuff. Keep it real this is my second motto keep it real. I tell at-risk teenagers about my experiences to help stop them from making the same mistakes. We all know some people have to lay their nose in horseshit to see if it really stinks. Real life experiences really matter to me and how I reach others is through my testimony. I share the truth and light on what a lot of people fear. I am not afraid of me. I am who I am, mainly to be somebody. No money in the world can make you happy if you are not aware of the spender. I am verging to earn the right to an NAACP Award or Essence Image Award. I probably told too much of my business so they may keep me off the ballet. Oh well, I am worth more than that. The way I feel about me, no award, certificate, public service announcement and dinner for two coupons can validate how special I already know I am. If you do not understand who you are, where you are going in life, as I stated before if you don't have a plan how can you let the little people watching your every move look up to you? Walk with so much patience, joy, determination despite the down days. You will get back up and you will appreciate your struggles for allowing you to fall. Eventually you will realize that it will be all right and when trouble comes your way, you will except it with open arms and embrace the storm. Then you will have a story to tell, then another and another. I am in the process of moving up and on my way; I look down as a constant reminder of two things. One, I look to remind me of the space I occupied and know that I can go back from where I came; and two I thank Jesus, for the successful yet painful journey to advance to the next level. We all want to impress those we encounter and some just don't give a damn, nappy hair, toes having a full conversation with you, color coordination all wrong, shoes, well let's say your heel is lower on one side and stand strong on the other. Let us get it together. I love to dress nice and being a big girl should not allow me not to. I can put a fit out together with every color on or off the rainbow. Earth tone colors fit my complexion, red is my favorite, and a splash of leopard print describes my mood the majority of the time. Personally my dress code was always on time, however when I was bickering with who did not love me I neglected everything around me including myself. You know what I am talking about, trash piling up, dishes ready to wash themselves, and blunt aroma in the air masked by cheap incense. All you have to do is get up and clean up that nasty ass house. If your dress game is tight and your house is filthy then you are in need of help. When you know who you are and what you are dealing within, the external will foster a glow. When you feel good, you look good so clean up that damn house! I remember sitting around the house with the shades folded, dark as hell, TV on but I am not watching it, laying down majority of the day in the fetal position halfway to sleep from crying over a sorry ass man for whatever reason. I got tired of dishes piling up. I was tired of the swollen eyes, the gaining of the weight, hollering at my kids for no apparent reason. I was tired of smoking from the break of dawn to the next. I got up, got out, and cleaned up my act. I realized that I had two little people who would one day be women themselves and now was the time to prepare that path for the shoes they were already playing in. Mine! It was time for me to set the right example for my mini divas. Tell that brother/sister to get a job, a career, go to school and further his/her education. Do something. It is not okay for a man to lie around and not have a job. If my man is lying around he is relaxing after a long hard day's work or he is off with PTO {paid time off}. Shit, my time is now. I have to live for myself first in order to be there for others. Therefore, with years far and beyond before, I become a grandmother; I would want my kids to use better mama nurturing skills to love their children. Deep inside we want to be the best, but to some our best is not enough. Handle what you know is comfortable and what pleases you. Not to say no one else matters, but if the situation was changed I would hope it would be an even swap no swindle. It will be better just to analyze your plan so your objective can creep right through on God's time. If no one else knows, He does. You will feel it, enjoy it when it hits, keep the feeling and do not forget to pray.

IN THE MORNING

He left around 1:00 am, limp body, eyes dazed, heart pounding for more. The rhythm we shared is like bass from a drop top Cadillac. When he leaves to go home, I am sick as a baby wanting him, wondering if his thoughts are of me as mine are of him. Is it true that you can spend too much time together, Hell yeah! We all need a break from one another, even from ourselves. Do not smother the brother/sister, and playing games with him/her either. Remember when he/she calls after 24 hours of space and he/she wants a run down on how your day was and you use the old line, "me and the girls/boys went to the club." Just let their ass go and concentrate on you. They will be back. For what it's worth, a man is attracted to a woman with spunk (vice versa), not the "I don't care" attitude. We do have to lay the rose petals down and let them sniff the aroma they may miss. If you know you are good scent then the aroma will forever tantalize his/her nose. Remember a rose is still a rose.

RESISTANCE

You try so hard to not say don't go, please stay, spend the night, just five more minutes. Hold back on being so aggressive. Sometimes our mates have places to go, things to do or just need time for them. If the brother/sister has blown your mind with his/her fancy techniques in bed and all you want to do is jump his bones, then nine times out of ten, he wants the same thing. So stop overreacting. If it were destined for you to be together, you would be. Relationships desire the emotional, social and spiritual attributes to combine two people alike and those who differ to prosper. In my opinion, some men do not tend to be as willing as females to set things off. Some not all are capable of handling an aggressive woman. It is important to give them what you would want in return. If things are not for the benefit of the both of you then move on. Time and energy can be wasted sometimes, but endure pleasure and pain before we come to the realization of what a relationship is supposed to be.

HATERS

I know people that sit at the crib all day long plotting how to bring some one else down. This book as I stated is for all of you. The ones doing the plotting and the ones plotted on. The bottom line is as simple as 1, 2, and 3. Someone is not going to like what you doing, how you dress, what kind of car you drive, and the man on your arm. Like, I told the babies I worked with as long as you know the person inside of you, then it should not matter what anyone else says or thinks of you. Self-acceptance can be very scary. We can work a lot harder on loving our haters instead of feeding fuel to the already blazing fire. God knows we have other issues to alleviate on our already full plates. Do not waste time on who dislikes you or even who do. I love them all no matter what. No, it does not mean I have tea and crumpets with them. I am not saying that, I keep a distance and do my thing. Just the way they like it. My heart will forever pump love and it is as simple as that. Put your time and effort into what is important YOU, and then loving others and especially your enemies will be simplistic and

the bible way!

MO DRAMA

I am transporting students on my company's van to after school and as I approach Beatties Ford Road and Tate Street, two Silly African American girls were fighting. One fired a shot at the other and chaos erupted. My first words to my kids were to get down! One of fighters looked as if she should have been a participant in a youth program and the other should have been in somebody's styling chair getting her skull decorated. I wish I knew the irony of it all, I assumed it was one of three things; a sorry ass man, he says she say, or money. Now I can feel all of this, but you must know how to handle the situation at hand without losing control. I had just recently got out of a relationship with a person that I was digging a lot. Every time I turned around, I was arguing with her, her and her. Over my sorry ass so called man. Every one knew of the relationship this person and me had. I felt good with him we looked good together. We made plans to do big things with and for one another. Nevertheless, he wanted to play around with the neighborhood chicken heads instead of coming home. Yeah, I am talking about the same lame that asked for steak, green beans, brown rice, and crescents. He had a gleam in his eye that let you know he was about to tell a lie. I loved this man dearly. I enlightened him, wined him and dined him, and showed him the finer things in life. However, that still was not enough to keep him dedicated to me and only me. When he finally got a job, the money went to the child support payments and $15.00 every Tuesday for the domestic violence classes at the McLeod Center against another woman. He would fill the chicken heads up with lies and unbelievable passion as he did me. In and out, my door became a revolving exit and entrance with him and his belongings. We have all done the foolish thing put him/her out and take him/her back repeatedly. The only thing that was good about the relationship was if he had, I had. He disrespected me by hitting me, lying, and cheating and being dedicated to him was not being respectful to my mini divas. Females got bold yawl and were calling my crib hanging up and playing silly games. He would hide his pager so I would not hear it beep or feel it vibrate. You can tell I have been writing this for a minute because pagers were in when I was dealing with him. Females would walk past the house as if they were going to the store 20 times a day to see if they could catch a sneak peak. I wondered were he was when no one walked passed. While he was with them, I tossed and turned wondering if he was making her feel, the way he made me feel. Shit if he was home girl was straight for the rest of the week. The entire ordeal was not worth the fussing, fighting or the headaches, the lost wages, the chasing him with weapons, and even telephones thrown at me. One evening we got in to it so bad after a male friend I had just met, whom I will introduce to you in the married man part of the book. I bet you are saying "Vonda you were not keeping it real." Well I was but the relationship was ending so I was open for conversation. Regardless of the situation count to 10, count 10 pennies, breath, relax, and shake that devil off your back. Drop to your knees and pray for a better day. Even, if it requires you being by yourself for a minute. Do you!

BEING ALONE

Some of the biggest fears of being a black woman are not getting what we need, needing companionship, the listening ear, someone to cook for, someone to clean after, quit tripping you know you want to fold up some boxers and mate up his socks, someone to love and to love you back. Thinking back on a lonely period in my life, I realized that I was never alone. I had family, friends, and co-workers who cared a great deal about who I was and how I felt. So what was the problem? I figured I wanted someone's attention in a romantic way. I was still on this self-discovery trip, which I was lacking in the pampering department towards myself. Remember what I said earlier, you are the center of someone's eye. You will never know if you do not show yourself the love and affection you desire. So treat yourself to some fresh cut flowers, a bottle of wine or even a bubble bath with smooth background music and a mirror to enjoy who you are. You will only settle for what you allow to keep you lonely.

MARRIED MEN

Do not let all of that loneliness lead to you to someone else's man or husband. It is not worth death, prison time, or a scarred reputation. Not over any man, I say, as I was setting up shop, in the process. I met a ball player and I will not reveal the sport or team, but I will say this motherfucker was married with a child and still is. I just could not understand why wifey called me with all the drama, if she was not going to leave his ass. I had to look back over the times I let the revolving door of mishaps enter my doorway. I told him good in the beginning; "let me know what is up with you and anyone you may be dealing with." He said, "Nobody but a baby mama." I told him if anyone calls, I was going to take her down the yellow brick road and through Alice's Wonderland so do not lie to me. He did not, therefore, she called and I spilled the beans on that ass. He did not bother to wear a ring or did not tell me he was married. I Prepared dinner for him and took it to his job every night. Homeboy did not have problems with greasing the palm for the bills to be paid. He put in a great deal of quality time and made me feel as if he was the one, until my sister Nita called and said on my answering service to call her as soon as I took my shoes off and sat down. The news that homeboy was married left me heartbroken and in disbelief. After several months of separation from this demon of deceit, I fell into his trap again. I led my stupid ass back into his arms once again. The moral of this story comes shortly after I realized I was working paycheck after paycheck, bills were piling up and I needed and wanted things, my car was about to blow up. I had the hardest time trying to trade that raggedy shit, until I left his ass alone for good. Things started to lift for me because I was no longer sinning with a sinner. I felt betrayed due to the fact the brother took it upon himself to think for me. Trying to make sense of the matter was my only concern. If I had known he was married, he would not have gotten anything but a smile and a rejection on top of that. That was and still is against what I value. It was unfair for him not to discuss being married. The anniversary of the day we met was approaching when I found out about his wife. He did not appear to be married, what does a married man look like? You might look for a ring. He did not wear one nor did a tan represented one exist. He stayed out late and was very visible with me in the public eye. Again, I was left confused, hurt all over again. Oh, well another one bites the dust.

MILLION DOLLAR LADY

A man expressed to me his feelings on the obstacles he was experiencing. He told me how much he admired me for moving out of the PJ's of Piedmont Courts and still doing the damn thing. I may not have the million bucks but I feel like I do. My life feels so crisp and never ending. I know from the many folks who congratulate me on my success that their believing in me moves me up the scale closer to the next level. Let me explain to those who think it is easy to move on up. Having low self-esteem, no one to share feelings with, being a single mom with baggage was a tough mountain to climb. However, through prayer and determination I made it happen. In spite of the drama, I did it. It was a blessing to live a better life and I am grateful for the opportunity to continue to do my best. It lets me see that someone other than my kids is watching, I mean a lot to many people so my best must be better, what about you? Are you going to settle for less, rather have what you deserve?

MAKING LOVE... THE PASSION

Has someone remarkable ever touched you and your knees buckle, the feeling that took you back to middle school on your first crush? Has that special someone who sends chills down your spine ever kissed you and made your panties wet? Has someone held you and your internal melts as your external holds on to the mushy frame that is supposed to support you? One thing I am pleased with is the way I enjoy love. Love is unique in everyone; love is different for everyone, the joy of kissing, being loved by someone, being happy and shocked out of my mind is the way I have been by one person, I will remain nameless. My days and nights were like walking on clouds. Have you ever met a person who smiled so perfect, laughed at all of your jokes, catered to your every need, satisfies your wants? Someone who caresses your thoughts, massages your feelings deeper and deeper for them? I am not getting ready to turn this into but or what if, rather I will say. Claim him! I did. No one is perfect. I am not and neither are you.

TENDERS

No, I am not talking about a 5 piece from Burger King. I am talking about the 19-25 year olds. Now I cannot speak for all the tenders in the world, but I can speak for the ones I have dealt with and the ones who are experiencing drama. Remember people, No more drama. Tenders are like newborn pups. Wet behind the ear, naïve to so much, neglected by those they care for, and hunching on anything. Tenders usually stay with their mothers, do not have a whip, and are low on cash. They tend to be smooth talkers, have a keen eye and a strong back. For those of you who cannot relate this is what is in store. "Let me break it down in its purest form," like comedian Tone-X says. When tenders approach you, they hit you with the OG lines, knowing they have yet perfected the game. As they make you laugh you squeeze your legs together as you admire his chest, legs, the gloss on his lips after that Tyrese lick he puts on them. The eye he gives you is watching every move and expression you make. The language you feed him alerts him of what to do with the next female he meets after you give him your business card with all of your contact information. Once the dinner is devoured, the dessert spills all over you, ice cream, mm's, caramel, hot fudge, fruit cocktail, topped with whipped crème and a plump cherry. After you have fucked up your mattress, pussy swollen, thighs aching, and mind, well let us say you have fucked up again. He is constantly at the door ringing your bell. Soon shoes, clothes, bicycles, CD's, cologne, and a set of weights have moved in with you, along with him of course. Promising to look for a job and would slap you upside the head for not dressing right, looking too sexy, talking on the phone too long, being gone for a minute longer than discussed all because he wanted a reason to stay with her all night. Ladies I had to put the shit in park, put his ass out and lock the car door turns up Aquemini by OutKast and put one in the air, a blunt that is. I did not need that drama, that extra heartache or stress. I flipped the disc and turn on Mary J. Blige from the 411 on up to NO MORE DRAMA. Let it out the way I knew best and let my troubles evaporate in the smoke. We have mission to complete. Would you like to be in a relationship where your mate loves you and only you? Were he pays the bills, massages your temples and toes, goes to church and keeps your heart dancing? Hey! I want to make history, now work on it. We are going to seek, find, and lose when it comes to our many affairs the heart will experience. One day we are going to conquer the black man and please people rule #1 pray for what you want # 2 treat him right. Do not go into the relationship with game. The ultimate rule of them all is to wait on God. With Him, we cannot go wrong. Remember what you put in is what you get out of it.

Are you guilty of smiling at him after his numerous attempts? Finally, you slip and bump your head on something very hard. Knowing you cannot see him when you want to. They have one thing the tender does not, a Job! Therefore, you know his woman, the kids, and the house is first come first serve. You will not see someone admire you two together as a couple. Therefore, he creeps over to your house on the late night making you jump out of bed at the sound of the doorbell. Until you get tired of going down 16 steps in the wee hour stiff hoping not to fall, so finally give him a key that he keeps hidden in the left hand side of his glove compartment. He gives the kids coins for the ice cream truck and buys a few pair of tennis pumps and you think you have it going on. How, when shit falls at his crib and he moves in with you and the only thing on his mind is his next victim. We cannot keep setting ourselves up. When you go into a relationship, know whom you are dealing with. As he is telling you shit that sounds good in the beginning and then the drama unfolds you start to remember what mama use to say, "take your time girl, take your time." Take a deep breath and put that on a shelf to rot. Not as a trophy, that is a piece worth keeping. Do not forget about your friend's man that just has to smell the panties. Not Lawrence Tipp, now that's a man that has kept it real in my eyes. There was a low down City of Charlotte worker coming to my crib pretending to want water. Faking the funk with conversation with their drama and pushing up on me. Even went as far as to drop his dirty ass pants in the middle of my living room floor as I am sorting out bills. I am trying to figure out how to make ends meet and get into a new car at the same time. In addition, he stands there flashing money that will take me out of my state of depression. Still the answer is no! How dare you? I love her. She is my ace, my dog, and my up when I am down. Get the hell on while I continue to figure out how to make ends meet. Paying bills, buying clothes, feeding the family, was the only issue at hand. Ladies we do not mess with our friends' men. Even if we do not consider them as friends, but communicate in some form or fashion. No, Hands off! Put him in his place and keep pressing on.

PAIN

Slamming dishes, doors, tearing clothes, cutting out zippers in Durango boots, putting hot sauce on a cream colored $180.00 Polo sweater, tearing shirt collars, smashing windows, breaking all of his shit up because you are pissed off. You feel that you have to get him back for making you feel this way. Ask yourself is it worth it? Then he has the nerve to call his sister to tell her to whoop your ass. Stop the madness I have been there, done that too. Men can unleash the beast only if you allow them to. You will turn into a regular Dr. Jekyll and Mr. Hyde. Again, is it worth it? If this has happened to you and you are still with him, 9 times out of 10 his ass has or will cause some shit to happen again, only this time different situation, different lady, (maybe, maybe not), but same pain. Is it worth it? An incident that happened that I will never forget is when my ex's friend of the family introduced my family member's, family member to my ex. This is not complicated, so pay attention. I came home from work one day and my ex-boyfriend

and all of his belongings had vacated the premises. At the time I
had no car so I called old faithful, the local cab company. From my
house to the house I expected and he was at was approximately,
$3.00 and some change to be exact. When I got out of the car, I
asked the driver to remain. I went up the seven steps that led to the
large neatly kept porch. The porch light was not on, but the blaring
sound of Keith Sweat's "Nobody" was serenading the atmosphere.
To this day I cannot stand that song. I knocked on that damn door
until the song went off. Finally, he peeks out. Now this is the funny
part. Because of the tint that was on the storm door, standing on
the porch as the person wanting in without the porch light on I am
only a silhouette. So dumb dumb unlocked the screen door and I
barge in. "What the fuck is going on in here?" I screamed, and
then the mystery woman comes around the corner fixing her pants,
"You nasty bitch!" I said. Someone I knew very well, someone kin
to my daughter. My next move was to the bedroom for evidence to
see the pulled back comforter and the messed up sheets that
adored the passion that shared amongst one another. He blocked
the door as if he was trying to save my feelings, "dude give me my
key" as he tried to explain, I grabbed my key and went to the right
towards the bathroom. There laid a used face cloth and the aroma
of hot sex and soap filled the air. We passed our words and I left. I

ended up back at home with a six pack of beer a blunt and some slow jams that only brought on more tears and pain. Love do not love nobody I said continuously after that incident, however pain brings change.

LOVE AFFAIR IN THE WORKPLACE

You know many jobs insist on employees not having intimate relationships. Well what they did not know did not get me fired. No one knew of the secret affair I had with a special someone on the job. I am not even going to say what job it was, but he is still an active part of my life. I can truly call him friend. This magnificent individual is like a homeboy to me, someone I can watch a football game with, ride out of town with and call on when I need to talk. He is that someone that massages the stresses away and always makes me smile. He believes in God and is a humble man. I am so proud of his accomplishments and I want some of his mother's potato salad. (Smile) Thanks, you know who you are for being the man every man should be. In no way am I encouraging workplace relationships, but if you can handle it do you, if not please settle for what God has for you, because that can be dangerous territory, emotionally, financially and you can loose a friend, a true friend if only you remained just that, FRIENDS.

JUST DO IT!

We all wish to be rich and to have the handsome buff, educated and well off man in our life. We want the perfect kids, house, and basic necessities of life. We also want that feeling we desire when we overcome, that feeling that exuberates within us when we made it and the good feeling it brings. What are you going to do about it? What is the hold up, him, your job, your kids, your friends, your habit, or you? Hey, that is it. So what are you going to do about it? What are you going to do to make shit happen? Shit sitting around waiting on the National Guard to escort Ed McMahon with the million dollar check, wipe the cold out your eyes. We all know our chances of the prize patrol knocking at Tom Tom and Shelia's door with a bouquet of roses and a Colt 45 bottle to celebrate their early retirement. I have not seen it. Well until you get that knock at your door, make a plan, set your goals, analyze your strategy, do it and watch it grow. Oh yeah, do not forget to pray.

QUESTIONS

When are we going to put our words into action?

When are we going to put our time to work?

If he said he will, she will because he said.

Why is it that we can't live our dreams, but

Mesmerize dreaming of others?

Being twenty-four hours in a day minus eight to sleep

What am I going to do with the rest of my time?

What are you going to do with yours?

Are we in a mixed up world or are we messed up

Within ourselves?

You have to get up get out and do something

Don't let the world pass you by. You have to get up get out

And do something its' your life.

We have people of many ages, watching every move we

Make From young to old you are in control of your

Achievements, what about your mistakes?

Do you accept the struggle or do you cry over every cup of

Milk that falls to your mailbox full of bills to your

Car catching spills of oil you slip on.

Have you fallen or do you get up?

You have to get up get out and do something

Don't let the world pass you by

You got to get up get out and do something it's your life.

With the decision I made to change my life style, I knew the responsibility lies within me and it was up to me to make a difference first with me in order for this change to come about. Every day we deal with people, in work, play and through contemplation. I figured through what mama taught me, common sense, book smarts, street smarts, and a combination of life learning experiences I should be okay. However, I was not all right. I was afraid to change. As long as I endured toxic environments, people and things, I was subjecting myself to staying the same. I later analyzed that I was not afraid to change I was afraid to fail. Today I am a better person from realizing no one is perfect. Life is like a science project sometimes it works out for the best result possible and then at times it does not. Perfecting this game was not easy and knowing how to cope when the bad times hit was something else to conquer. Eventually something worse would bind to TRY to tear me down, or was it me? Change is not going to knock on everyone's door, we all have to change our sheets right? (I hope). So do not wait for the change master to complete the speech before you decide why it is important.

Here are some helpful quotes that inspired my direction toward change.

"Nothing worth while comes easily. Work, continuous work and hard work, is the only way to accomplish results that last".
By: Hamilton Holt

"Do what you can, with what you have, where you are."
By: Theodore Roosevelt

Make it happen today so tomorrow can be a day to remind you of how good it feels to have changed.
By: Ms. DeVondia Roseborough

METAMORPHOSIS

Webster's New World Dictionary states the meaning of *Metamorphosis is a marked change of character, appearance, condition, etc.*

You have just gone down the yellow brick road and through Alice in Wonderland on a journey full of attitude, hurt, anger and frustration. I still reminisce off my all time favorite Mary J. Blige CD, My Life. I still wanted someone to share my world and be free of the drama in my life. I no longer smoke weed or drink. I bet you are curious how I changed. Well I went from a size 26 to a size 14; I now wear contacts instead of glasses. I have been with the YWCA from June of 1995-December of 2003. Before I get to December 9, 2003 let us get on the throwback train. Remember Jermaine, yeah the love of my life. The one I took home to meet mama. The one I am still seriously in love with. Boy did we share some good times. Lunch at Bellacino's, Black Bean Soup at TGIF Friday's, a peace of mind at McDowell Park, the smooth sounds of the Isley Brothers at

The Cricket Arena, scallops, shrimp, oyster, salmon patties, orange Kool Aid, roses, cards, emails, quality time, love, and sweet conversations. Boy do I love him. He inspires me to keep being the best I can be in spite of any obstacle and situation. He is always humble and there when I need him. My job was going great. My cousin Poo Poo told me she has never met any one that liked their job as much as I did. I had students who listened to the words that rolled off my tongue. F's and D's turned in to A's and B's, 8th grade students on 5th grade reading levels improved beyond their grade expectations. Hip Hop Cultural contest winners in both spoken word and creative design; sponsored by the Mecklenburg Council on Adolescent Pregnancy. For two years in a row, I had students win the Do the Write Thing Essay Challenge Con-test. One National and two represented as local winners. In addition, one student represented Mecklenburg County's Student of the Year for the North Carolina Support Our Students Program. I started as a substitute teacher in a Daycare in the Piedmont Courts community, to Site Director / Team Leader for the Y's after school programs and summer camp for middle school-aged youth living in at-risk areas. Through meeting countless people and sharing many adventurous trips and activities with the youth and young adults, I took my job very personal and serious. Each student I encountered I took the time to know everyone. Some of the students even lived with me from time time. I was there home away from home. With this wonderful job, I was able to clean up my credit to buy my first home, a three bedroom, bath and ½ flat in the Oakview Terrace Community. Something we do not take serious, our credit and all that money renting instead of investing in home-ownership. Known to many as Creektown, back in the day, the neighborhood was nowhere you wanted to be. Drugs, violence, and trouble embarked on the ones that struggled to get by. Even though the neighborhood is not the Hampton, it has upgraded since Habitat for Humanity started building single family homes for those who desire to live better. I said goodbye to Piedmont Courts and hello to the newly revital-ized First Ward Place Town homes, which used to be the old Earle Village Community, back in the day. I lived there for seven months. Always with a back up plan, I had filled out the paper-work and completed the home-owner's classes through Habitat for Humanity and November 7, 1998 I said hello to my own home. The home DeVondia and the volunteers of various organizations and churches helped my girls have with a big backyard. Getting down to a size 14 from a 26 was not easy. Consistent walking, drinking of water and watching what I ate made a difference. I started to feel like change was coming even with out me initiating it. My way of thinking, talking, the clothes I wore as well as the company I kept became obsolete. I even purchased a 92 Sedan Deville and paid it off in 2 years minus two years on the sales contract. Life was great or was it?

JANUARY, 2003
_____

I caught the flu after having a common cold for weeks. I
came home from work daily as if I had helped build a skyscraper
in the uptown district. I would slam my weary body down on the
bed as soon as my purse and backpack hit the floor. My late night
conversations with my best friend had ceased. Half the time I did
not even hear the phone ring. What was going on with my favorite
sitcom show was nothing to ask me about anymore, my housework
had slacked off and my full course meals had turned into TV
dinners, ham & cheese sandwiches, and oodles of noodles. I did not
know where my energy had gone. My days and nights consisted of
being fatigued, an irritable attitude, a dirty house and a child out of
order. I was missing so much; I felt I was loosing it. I did not
understand why Jermaine was not spending as much time with me
as before. I still had the same feelings as I had always felt for him,
but I was missing the conversations and seeing him everyday like I
used too. He no longer worked in my city, so we would communi-

cate by phone or email. However, when we were able to see one another we made up for lost time. Oh! I failed to mention that Jermaine lived with his baby mama down south. No, I did not luck up on finding out. He did what he was supposed to do. He told me. However, I chose to get involved with him any ways. I had no problem with it and nor did I cause any, do not judge, just listen. After going through what I had gone through with all the other relationships, I decided why not. Everything was just the way we wanted it, until I wanted more. As I began talking about the many things, I wanted out of the relationship that was not going to be I went ahead and settled for what it was. I was cool with it, I guess. Even though he completed me at least that was the way, he made me feel. I trusted him for being honest with me and I respected my decision for what I chose to do. However, something was still not right with me.

THE JOURNEY

I remember when I had my first child I was told I was anemic, (a deficiency of red blood cells). The balls of my feet were like ice and I continued to catch colds and had hard times trying to rid them. I placed the blame once again on the public service I provided day to day, shaking hands and telling kids to cover their mouths when they sneezed. After numerous trips to the doctor and her too agreeing with my iron being low prescribed pills and a multi-vitamin to see if it would help. It did in some ways with the boost from the Red Bull Energy Drink. I only got worse health wise, but before I get there let me take you on a journey called preparation. The journey that helped me deals with the many issues of attitude and strife. I started feeling brand new. I thanked God more often than I ever did before. I felt myself getting closer to him through His strength not mine alone, as an obedient child I followed. I began praying more and appreciated my struggles more than ever before. I asked him to guide me through and prepare me for what ever came my way. That way of thinking puzzled me, but I did not dare question him why. My 32nd birthday came October 8, 2003 and I had experienced many lightheaded feelings. Feeling as if I were about to faint. Not until November did I start to pass out. The funny thing is I would pass out in the same spot at the same time every morning in my kitchen getting ice from the freezer. Each morning I woke up at 5:00 AM gown drenching wet in sweat thirsty for water and ice to cool me. When I would come to I would awake with a smirk on my face saying, "What in the hell!" Laugh it off, Get up, get my kids and myself ready for the day, and not disclose anything that had happened. Thanksgiving I slept most of the day at my mama's house. I still did not know what was going on. I fainted several more times until I could not risk being behind the wheel of my car with my kids or someone else causing harm or death. I went to the Urgent Care Clinic to see a doctor, at that time a white coating had took over my tongue causing my breath to make a dog bow down. If you notice something different about a person that is not normal for them, like stinking breath, please tell them. Many people, even on my job did not even tell me my breath was on fire. Laughing behind my back and talking amongst one another, I knew that was the case. Its' not what you tell it is how you deliver the information. I even asked

Jermaine at a Charlotte Hornets against the Los Angeles Lakers game did my breath stink. He said no of course. Thrush not only made my breath smell, but it made hot sauce hotter than hot and ice cream was like hot sauce on the tongue. When I brushed my tongue, the mildest toothpaste caused painful side effects. Given a medication, called Diflucan to treat the infection called thrush, a fungal infection in the mouth. I took many tests, blood samples, and urine analysis and stool samples that I had to take over a course of 3 days and take to the lab for testing. I prayed and asked God to let every thing be all right. I infected with the HIV virus was the feeling I had for a while. My best friend said she believed I knew from the doctors telling me all along, I knew from when all else came back, nothing was wrong in that department, sit back and listen to God. I became a listener for a change and my direction was steered into a new path of the unknown. This feeling was from God. God did not give me the virus, my irresponsibility did. He allowed me to see through the forest filled with smoke and weeds. If you feel what I am saying clap one time, now keep reading. A feeling of peace is what I felt. Remember when I said He started to allow things to happen to me and how I accepted what came my way. I acted on that gut feeling and became able to accept what ever the results read. During this change in my health, I became bright in spirit. I got along better with others and my attitude was changing for the better. My God was and had prepared me for the December 9, 2003 results. I asked my cousin Lashawn to accompany me after the doctor called me on my cell phone at work and asked me to report to the office as soon as possible. My stomach was on butterfly control. When we arrived, I waited nervously flipping through magazine after magazine. When the nurse called my name, the lump in my throat grew larger. I was in the same exam room as the week before. The doctor arrived shortly and told me all of my tests came back great except for one concern. I took a deep breath, looked at the blood pressure pump on the wall and moved my eyes slowly up the wall as the clock struck 10:12 AM December 9, 2003; I had a positive HIV test. As he said this, he placed his hand on my right knee. Feeling numb is all I can remember. I had no feeling of who, what, when, or where, but I knew how. He prescribed me some medicine and told me to contact my primary physician as soon as possible. Still I was numb. He told me that people are living longer with the disease, unlike before, to seek care promptly. I thanked him as I shook his hand and proceeded out the door. My cousin was on the phone as I walked out to the waiting area. She asked, "What did he say?" I replied, "He told me I have HIV!" "What!" She spoke loudly as she told the person on the phone she would call them back. Still I had no tears for the information that had unfolded before me. I had No feelings none what so ever. We went to Show Mars a couple of blocks down because I was hungry. We ate and talked about the news. I was not in disbelief and was prepared, for my new beginning. I gleamed at the food my cousin had purchased and commented on how good it looks. She asked me if I wanted some, I said no. I could not bring myself to eat off her plate. The stigma had set in on me already. People you cannot get HIV from eating off another person's plate, using there toilet or comb or brush. She insisted that I eat a piece of her Gyro and stop being petty. That we were family and we could share food off one another's plate. My cousin told me she was amazed at how well I was handling it all with her big dark eyes laced in tears. "Do not be a punk" Was all I could say. I called a friend; she was having lunch with her mother. All I could hear was No! screaming from the phone. I called my best friend and she thought I was playing a sick joke. I called my other best friend Tipp last. She had a fit, ready to fight, cussing like a sailor. "Who girl who is it?" "I don't know! I just was slipping on that oil. I said. Caught up in the moment and contracted the HIV virus." After LaShawn and I ate we went over to a friend of ours and got me some green and a Dutch Master and went back to my house. My cousin tells me still to this day that all I did was rock back and forth saying, "Don't cry! I don't want anyone crying for me." As I am saying this, she is trying to fight the crocodile like tears that have already stained her jeans. My best friend burst through the door and immediately tries to console me. She and her mom assured me that whatever it takes to get me right and keep me right would happen. I called Jermaine to let him know. He could not believe what I had said to him. He immediately let me know that we were in this together and we both had a past. I had taken two HIV test that year and both were negative. I insisted on going to see my doctor, so my cousin and I took a ride to the clinic. I walked in to my doctor's office bumping right into her as I got off the elevator and broke the news to her. She expressed her deepest sympathy and immediately scheduled me the first available appointment, which in my favor was the next day. After I had gotten home I rolled my blunt smoked it all up by myself, and rocked back and forth. I laid the three page report on my pillow. This report neatly compiled every test given and explanations for each one. The front page read at the bottom right hand corner POSITIVE HIV 1 test. I remembered the doctor saying they would run the HIV 2 test for confirmation. No response indeed I was positive and hoping when I woke up from the dream I was having that instead of that paperwork on my pillow would be the beams of the sun instead. I smacked the pillow and screamed out, "Lord Why!" Even with that blunt, I woke up to the same issue I laid down with. I continued to pray my continuous prayer, "Dear Lord, please guide me, don't let me die. Allow me to be strong and grant me more patience and the ability to be obedient to you."

WHY

I continued to suffer fainting spells, dizziness, and fatigue. Why was the question that never left my mind? I knew that it took two people that made a bad choice in engaging in unprotected sex. I had not had a blood transfusion and I was not an IV drug user. I just was a careless woman with no respect for my mind, body and soul. Caught up in the heat of the moment and infected with the disease known as "As I Die Slowly." My mom, how was I going to tell my mom? I was not prepared to tell her the news of me having HIV. She has done everything in her power not to hurt my sister or me. How could I do this to her? How could I tell her? The question came back to mind again, why. I went to my mom's house and she was not there. My sister Teka was and I decided to confide in her. She hugged me and told me she loved me and was going to be there for me. I begged her not to tell mama and she promised. I went through the next few weeks with the Jada Kiss question continuously on my mind; you remember that song, WHY. In spite of it all, I became strong in my faith, which allowed me mentally to act normal. I was always the one to hold things together. Always the person anyone could come to for help. I went to work and followed what was expected. I continued to sleep a lot for the remainder of the month until December 31, 2003. I poured me the last of my Raspberry Vodka and toasted the New Year in with WPEG Power 98 and a prayer. After I woke up at 5:00 AM January 1, 2004, I thanked God for another year. I know I said previously that I had stopped drinking and smoking, but in the famous words of TC, I collapsed. (Laughing Out Loud) He meant relapsed when he told us at MasterKuts Beauty/Barber Shop that he had stopped smoking and started back again telling Toya he had collapsed. As I reached for ice to serve my again drenching in sweat, hot body, I fainted once again. This time I hurt my head on the hard floor in my kitchen. After I revived, I staggered back to my bedroom were I fainted once again across the footboard of my cannonball bed bruising my right thigh. Bouncing back was not a problem but this time I called my cousin and asked her to take me to the emergency room. This had never happened before and I was afraid at this point. After being in the Presbyterian Hospital emergency room for many hours with a 107 degree temperature, fever and hallucinating, my cousin told me I wanted the TV on Roseanne in the room they had me in, but no TV was there. I would remain for the next 23 days. Pneumonia, Macro bacteria Infection {MAC}, 7 blood transfusions, MRI's, Cat Scans, fluid drained from my lungs and kidneys. A Bone Marrow biopsy, plenty of chicken broth, family, friends, the wonderful Dr's and nurses who took care of me during this trying time. One Doctor in particular I must recognize is my Infectious Disease MD with ID Consultants in South Charlotte. Dr. Thomas Verville and his staff made sure I knew everything there was to know about the virus. Around the third or fourth day of my stay in the hospital, Dr. Verville came into my room to let me know that I had AIDS! I could deal with the HIV diagnoses but told I had AIDS was not what I wanted to hear. He placed his hand on my right knee as I replied, "No! I have HIV!" I do not know what came about but the tears that were ready to form in my eyes suddenly disappeared. The white doctor's coat he wore was whiter than I had ever seen before. This angelic touch was comforting and made me feel that everything was going to be all right. Dr. Verville's touch was like the feeling I got from the Doctor when he announced my results. I had a feeling of peace. If God was not with me, yawl had better shout praise the Lord right now. I saw Dr. Verville 3-4 times a day, always with a smile and his hand in mine. He greeted everyone that surrounded me during his visit. However, there is a HIPPA law and he made sure first, that everyone that was in the room with me respected my privacy by allowing me to make the decision on receiving information about my health in front of those around. An Angel is what he is to me. Someone on earth God placed before me as my guide through this crisis. My T cell count was 19, (T cells are white blood cells from the thymus, important to the immune system) which made me vulnerable to infections and possibly death. God was not through with me yet, He needed me here to write this book for you to tell some one else to buy it and read. He needs me to do other things to get the word out about the disease. Moreover, how it is affecting our communities, our lives and our nation. Remember when I asked the doctor, what do I do next? After the pneumonia and severe fevers, I dropped from weighing 198 pounds to 139 pounds in 20 days. I was truly ready to go home. I had a wonderful nursing staff. I must say they took good care of me. I felt helpless not being able to bathe myself and go to the restroom on my own. I was a helpless fragile woman who had still not shed a tear. The hardest part was waking up and my mom was on my left side of me asking how I was and why I could not come to her. I responded by saying, "I didn't want to hurt you." She replied, "It's going to be okay, just give it to God and let him take care of what he wants." She did not judge me, chastise or ridicule me. She jumped right in and took care of my family and me. I wanted to be home for the Panthers super bowl game against the New England Patriots. I teased all of the staff at the hospital the entire week about the Panthers coming out on top. I even told a nurse she could not take my blood because she was going for the other team. I was only playing. We all had a good time. I had so much blood taken from me that they eventually had to cut a centralized line in order for them to test my blood, every morning and every night. I had to receive oxygen to help me breath. If you had a cold, you could not visit. I was glad to go home on January 23, 2004. I immediately went right back on January 25, 2004 for two more blood transfusion and this time I stayed at Carolinas Medical Center. With the utmost kindness and respect from all, especially from... I cannot remember this young woman's name, but she was a brown-skinned medium build woman with the perfect smile. Every time she came to my room and asked me what I wanted to eat, she greeted me with a smile and a humorous and bubbly attitude. She seemed to be like me in many ways, she loved to make others smile and she loved her job and the people she served. She put me up on the real menu at the hospital, cheeseburgers and fries, no T-bone though. I still could not get it down as I wanted to, but it sure looked and smelled good. After my two-day stay, I was back at home this time for good. Free of fevers transfusions but now diarrhea and vomiting was an issue. I met Pastor WJ Neal, Pastor of Christ Missionary Church, during my stay at Presbyterian Hospital. I was surprised to see that he and his wife the former Ruby Cash who is a high school graduate of mine from Garinger High School class of 91 came by. My cousin Ebony Henderson (Miss. Punk) told me about the pair and they came by and prayed with me. I remember Pastor Neal telling me, "Have faith of a mustard seed. Telling me to say the Lord's Prayer, Psalms 23 and believe in what he said he would do." My mother had my great aunts from South Carolina to come up as well. My deceased Grandfather's sister, on my mother's side of the family and her Mother's sister. We had church up in there. They prayed and laid hands on me, brought the oil and sang hymns. The nurses were at the door and feeling the spirit that was in the room. Remember that infection that was on my liver, well because of that infection told that they would have to take my spleen out. The devil is a liar and the fever finally broke. During my time of recovery, I balanced my days, nights praying, and asking God to forgive me. I had Pastor Neal and his wife come in to pray with my girls, my Mother and Stepfather. I also asked him to come by and anoint my home to free it from the negativity that surrounded my family and me once I got home. My mother made sure I saw my children everyday but one while I was in the hospital. My children are like night and day, loveable, smart and vibrant personalities. Each handles situations differently. At home, my youngest daughter would be up under me, brushing my air to massaging my feet, while my oldest would confine herself to her room listening to music and playing the play station 2. While I hospitalized, the tables turned. My youngest would come in to speak but would go off down the hall to the family lounge and drink coffee in front of the TV, while her big sister greased my scalp, laced my lips with Vaseline, combed my hair and even clean out my sink in my room to arranging the flowers delivered by family and friends. The situation affected both of them in different ways. As you read further in the book, you will see how each one handled the news of my diagnosis. My oldest daughter started to wild out even more with her defiant attitude towards teachers and adults and people of authority. She crossed the line when she disrespected my mom and had to go to a group home for a month. That was hard for me, because on the day she departed for therapeutic care I was in the hospital handling that business over the phone.

MY FUNERAL ARRANGEMENTS

How many limos will I need? I started to visualize the long line of cars slowly creeping behind the hearse that carried my cremated remains. At this time I am sure everyone including myself is unsure about the outcome of my condition. I remained hopeful with good spirits, but at the time, I was writing my living will and seeking advice on powers of attorney. When I realized that people had themes for funerals my imagination created a celebration unlike those I have experienced and probably you as well. I planned a straight up down to earth fish fry. (LOL) I am dead serious, with words that strongly encouraged everyone to be him or herself as they celebrated my homecoming. Big speakers playing my favorite songs, wash pot fish that contained the best vegetable oil to cook not so big croaker that was golden brown and seasoned to perfection. Macaroni & cheese made by the third best because I was the second and my grandmother taught me so she was the best, coleslaw grated from firm heads of cabbage with Miracle

Whip, salt & pepper, fresh onions, a dash of sugar and a drop of vinegar and to wash it all down, T's Tea. My home girl Tipp's tea will make you drink it up in one gulp looking for the nearest pitcher for a refill. I wanted everyone to eat and drink. I love to feed people and see them smile while patting their bellies. With singing, dancing and laughing filling the atmosphere whiles my friends and family enjoyed memories of me. I stayed optimistic in healing and kept my faith in believing I was going home to get even better. At the same time, I was thinking ahead not wanting to leave my family with the agony of making arrangements. The word says when a baby is born you cry and when someone dies you rejoice. One thing is for sure I will not put a question mark were God has put a period, neither should you.

BUTTA

I received a phone call from Jermaine asking me to come to his place of employment. I asked why. He responded, "I have something for you and the girls." I was on vacation this particular day in April 2002, hopped in the car preceded to my destination. When I pulled up to park, he shouted from afar, "Pull around back!" I parked the car where he stood and got out. From nowhere a tiny brown puppy appeared. My eyes filled with tears and I shouted, "It is so cute, what kind of dog is it?" Jermaine said, "A mutt, do you want it?" A home girl of his wanted to get rid of it and gave it to him to give to somebody that would take care of it. I could not say no, to this big brown-eyed tan colored whatever kind of dog it was. Initially his name was Smiley. Let me explain no one knew what the sex of the dog was. She appeared to look like a male dog, I guess because she was so tiny and swollen in her genital area that we could not tell. Smiley was not my choice of name for him. Jokingly Jermaine said, "Well whatever it is you better take it or I am going to take her to the country and let her loose." "Not this puppy you won't!" as I scooped her up and walked towards the car while Jermaine placed the kennel in the back floor of the car. I hugged his neck and thanked him from the girls and I and he said, "I knew you would take care of it that's why I wanted to give it to you all." Smiley and I went to the after school program just in time for my kids were getting ready to board the van to come home. Bright eyes gleamed as if it were Christmas all while Smiley jumped from my arms. We took her home not knowing her sex and a name for her. So many crazy nouns and adjectives came out of our mouths until my oldest daughter said, "Mama you name him." Remember we still do not know he is a she. Before night came, Smiley had a new name Butta. I named her Butta because of her features that melted my heart. Her warm, silky two-toned brown and tan coat cuddled our lives and added needed smiles. We realized a few weeks later that Butta was a girl after my cousin Jeff came to inspect her. I remember my mother and grandmother saying that, "Two women can't stay in the same house." Butta chewed up several pairs of Timberland boots of mine. Destroyed my kids' tennis shoes, flip-flops and my favorite pair of bedroom slippers, it was time for home dog to go out side. A very protective puppy Butta was. I remember one time she was out on the front porch; at least I thought she was. She went smack dead in the middle of the street and had traffic backed up both ways in front of the house all I heard was car horns blowing like crazy, did Butta move? No! She sat there as if she was in charge of the avenue she lives on. Nose pointed straight up in the air as if she was the queen of the Bassets. Yes, Butter is a Basset mix. She looks like an over-weight weenie dog with a deep throaty bark. I made Butta a part of my memoir because she is family. Ice and snow was on the ground when I came home from the hospital on January 23, 2004. The doctor told me I could not be around any animals due to my weak immune system. That meant no fish for the fish tank, saying no to baby girl when she wanted a gerbil, planting flowers in my yard and touching my Butta! Don't touch my dog! Out of it all Butta made the tears flow. It was a cool morning and my mother had just gotten through feeding her. I came through my laundry room that connected to the side door. This was actually my first time seeing her since December 31, 2003. Butta turned into a teary fit when she saw me. Tears formed in my eyes as I beg my mom to let me talk to her while promising I will not get to close. Butta was not going for that, she wanted to feel me smooth her coat and make kissing sounds at her. Miss. Thing tore the screen up on the storm door trying to get at me. I did not get to touch her, knowing I still had to be careful of the germs. She cried and scratched yearning for me to rub her healthy thick Kibbles 'N Bits eating self. When my mother finally left for work one day after my second return home from the hospital I prayed a prayer, wrapped up tight in my blue plush Tommy Hilfiger robe my best friend and her husband got me, went outside and loved her like she wanted me to. I washed my hands and washed up with a smile. God did not bring me this far to give up on me now. I love you Butta!

BATH OR SHOWER

I was bedridden for a short time and could not bathe myself. Between my nursing staff, my best friends, my sister Teka and my mom I was so fresh and so clean. Weak and defenseless describes me trying to defeat the lack of strength for getting out of the tub. I later learned a woman living with HIV should not take baths because of the risk of catching unwanted infections. My mom on one side trying to lift 130 pounds was not a good look. Luckily, my Sister was there and certified in all branches of CNA. With her help and expertise I was successfully boosted from the human aquarium, all while tears filled my eyes as I saw the sorrow on my Mother's face as she left out not wanting me to see her face filled with pain. With the feeling of getting well and the determination to win this battle I continued to ask the Lord please hold on to me. Now getting out the shower was no picnic either. I had no strength to lift my leg over the tub to touch the floor. My legs felt as if it had 20 extra pounds on it because of it being wet. As I would slowly turn to rinse the lathered soap off my body I would get dizzy and very light headed. As I continued my exercises the physical therapist trusted me to do without her, she felt that I was going to recover and that spending my money was unnecessary because of my willpower. Therefore, she told me to call if I needed her and left me directions to follow on basic leg exercises. I regained my strength now with another issue to deal with. My showerhead had no ump to it. I needed that pressure to massage my body and caress my stresses away. I contacted a plumber for a few other things that needed to taken care of around the house. God sent who I came across to me. How can God send you a plumber? You might ask. I had not heard of him before and just simply let my fingers do the walking in the yellow pages of the phone book. Well, Mr. E.A. Jones Plumbing Services Co. came out and fixed everything in the first bathroom and through me in the new showerhead that massages in many adjustable settings. When he went into my bathroom, I knew he could see with the numerous items on display that I had just gotten out of the hospital. Just looking at me, I am sure he knew that something was wrong. I was dark in the face; I made small steps through out the house as I noticed him watching me as I moved slowly towards him, as he wanted me to take at look at the finished job. As I paid him, less than what I expected and took the receipt. He offered to pray with me. A very touching and profound moment and well worth reflecting back on. I told you God is great. Ahh you know it. He has done everything to send disciples on my journey even if it is only for 45 minutes to an hour. Everyone serves his or her purpose on your journey for a short time or for the long haul. For however long, do not dwell on it just thank God for the time spent and keep it moving.

MY HOME GIRLS

All of my closet friends have been in and through the storm with me. I mean they know how I am feeling from the tone of my voice to the swagger in my sway. Each one of these women holds a special place in my heart and I love them very much. I appreciate you all for standing in as mommies for my mini divas when I was down, helping me with finances and taking me out to lunch to fatten me up. For transporting me to my doctors appointments, applying for the Metrolina AIDS Project, talking to me long hours throughout the night. Thank you for massaging my feet, brushing my hair and just showing you care, volunteering with me at different HIV/AIDS fundraisers and events. You all are so special to me and I love you all so very much for all you put up with and do for me.

TOSSING AND TURNING

I had a hard time after I came from the hospital sleeping in my bed. For some apparent reason I was not comfortable and kept the TV on all night long. One night I lay in my bed and drifted off to sleep, at least I thought I was asleep to open my eyes and an image of a little blue elf similar to a Smurf said to me, "Turn over on your left side, you have dope in your butt." I was astonished to see with my eyes a blue image of a cartoon character on the left side of me. I was scared to death, real talk; I actually laid there for about two hours before I slowly turned my weak body over on my side on the devil's command, "Dope!" I screamed. What the Hell!" I screamed, "Mama!" I screamed to the top of my lungs waking her out of her sleep. "Look in my butt and see if you see any dope in it!" "Girl, I don't see anything you better call your doctor in the morning and check on the side affects of that medicine." She reminded me of the medicines making me hallucinate. That experience led me to the living room sofa, my mom into baby girl's room until my house anointed with oil, and prayer took place. My daughters, mother, stepfather and I gathered with my Pastor and his wife in the living room for prayer. He walked outside and down the hallway to every room and blessed the house for no evil lurked our space after that. Sister Neal prayed as Pastor Neal walked throughout the house and in the yard with the oil and I shook as tears rolled down my face as I felt the deliverance take place right before my family's eyes. After that, I took a long warm shower and my mother greased my body down with a lotion that finally penetrated my dry skin to relieve the roughness and the scaly look. I was able to sleep comfortably in my room. I slept so good my mattress felt as if Rooms To Go delivered it with extra pillow top comfort and plush forgiveness. My bedroom was full of a demon that is why I could not have a good night sleep. Getting my house and yard blessed, I felt the newness in my home, the spirit of God was in my place, why, because I was seeking close-ness with Him, and I could not do it with negative spirits around. It was not three months quite and I decided to go ahead and rid of the bedroom set that had been there and done that through the good and the ugly. Closure is what I call it. My supportive family and friends continued to come over day after day to check on my family and me. I had a home nurse to come in to help me as well with regaining strength and the use of my weak muscles. After two visits, she told me there was no need to waste my money because I was doing great without her. God was continuing to heal and motivate me faster than anyone expected. Do not question my Father's work, He knows best. My mama moved in with me preparing meals, shopping for the house and kids, getting them prepared for school and paying my bills. I was in a good situation going through this, being that I had a job with benefits I was able to get my hospital bills paid on time. Thank God, for (BCBS) Blue Cross Blue Shields of North Carolina. I had a case manager through BCBS named Ms. Virginia Thombs, RN, BSN, and CCN. She was the most amazing woman. She was so knowledgeable about my care. Ms. Virginia called me faithfully with information on how to care for my hair, emotional support to getting my Social Security Benefits started. Many thanks go out to you Ms. Virginia W. Thombs. My Short-term disability started to roll in on a weekly basis. Thanks to Scottie Chastain, Chief Human Resource person with the YWCA. She made sure my paper work done to perfection, signed dated and submitted on time with no delays. I truly believe no matter what position you hold whether it is with the Department of Social Services, working with children or flipping burgers if you truly want to help someone, everyone can receive the assistance they need. Thanks Scottie for being so caring and diligent in making sure no more added stress was upon me. My income taxes were filed and deposited into my account. I dipped in my retirement until my Long-term disability kicked in and shortly after I received my award letter for Retirement, Survivors and Disability Insurance benefits. I was living as though each day was my last. I was terribly afraid that I was going to die during a point all kind of thoughts were going through my head. Who was going to raise my kids? Who was going to listen to my best friend at 3:00 in the morning when things got rough? One thing for sure the world would be okay without me. One thing I do not advise is burning up your life savings, I had over 30,000 dollars in retirement once federal and state took their share I had about 20,000 to basically splurge on. I had lack of little faith and afraid I was going to die and wanted my last days on earth with my children to be memorable days for them. I learned that many did the same thing I had done those that are positive, after reading articles of scared infected persons spending their life savings and not dying and looking out a window to the heavens wondering how they are going to survive. Hold on to the loot and do not over spend. If you have faith, that faith of a mustard seed, God will see you through.

My Cadillac caught another attitude and I was depending on others to get me back and forth to my appointments. I thank every one that got me home safely. I do not mean any harm, but many of my friends cannot drive as well as I do. All of them dropped what they were doing to cater to my needs. Living with HIV requires a person to have lots of authentic loving and caring people around. On this particular day, I wanted not to rely on my friends, so I caught a cab to the beauty parlor with my daughter. I honestly had no business going to the salon at all. That was about a month after released from the hospital. Paying attention to my side effects was a priority but remembering was another issue. One of the many issues I suffered as I recovered, short-term memory. I felt due to the high fever made me lose knowledge of some things. I was glad to be out, I needed to be out, bad enough to do it in the snow that was dirty red due to the wintry mix that covered the city. I went to see my stylist LaToya Adams who possesses the golden touch. That woman can work a pair of Marcel in any dimension. My tresses are always silky smooth, healthy and compliments ring until the next week's appointment. This particular day sitting under the dryer for a prolonged period of time, which one of my medications requires me not to do so, left me fainting in the cell phone retail store next door. I had not eaten due to my unbalanced appetite and it was still hard to keep food down. I felt my knees wobble and bounce back and forth against the glass cabinet that stored cell phones and their accessories, I looked around to the right and saw my daughter look at me and she immediately asked if I was all right. A man in line ahead of me asked, "Lady is you alright!" As my daughter heads towards the door, she screams in horror taking off down the large corridor of the mall. All I recall is falling back with my pocketbook clutched tightly up under my arm with close to $900.00 in cash. Seeing me faint was a scary thing for her and me both. I came to rather quick and I immediately declined the ride back to the hospital. I gave it to God and thanked him for allowing me to realize that I had better sit my behind down somewhere. My stylist and I shared tears and laughed about the ordeal. I could not even pick up my crab legs on sale at the Winn Dixie. I know you are saying this fool is worrying about some crab legs. No I make the best out of any situation; rather it is good or bad. Try it some times. After Toya dropped us off at home, I called my doctor's office and the nurse confirmed that the heat from the dryer and not eating caused me to black out. Once I ate and laid down for a bit, I was back to my speedy recovery.

TO MY STYLIST

This is an essay contest that I entered my stylist in April 2004, sponsored by Sally's Beauty Supply. We did not win but remember what I said about a piece of paper defining whom or what we are.

December 2003 I found out, I was HIV positive. During this trying time, I was in the hospital for 23 days and received 7 blood transfusions. During my stay, LaToya Adams who is my stylist made numerous phone calls and paid me surprise visits, on one visit she accompanied with a yellow gift bag that carried a 9-inch pair of praying hands draped with a gold chain, which hangs a cross. The porcelain hands sat the entire time on my nightstand in the hospital and to this day at home, I display it on my dresser. During my time of illness, my stylist who performs creative designs to my short tresses provided hairdos in spite of my financial ability to pay. Toya provided me with transportation to and from the salon. She treats me the same regardless of the diagnosis. Not only do we have a great time reminiscing the days we shared in high school, but also we take an occasional lunch with one another. My hair is treated, washed, set and styled by the one who possess the Golden touch. Sharing laughs and even tears is apart of Toya's character. Toya is a dedicated friend and stylist. Her warm kindness attached to her beautiful smile is indeed the owner of the Golden Touch. For this reason above is why I feel Toya Adams is this years "Golden Touch" recipient.

I wrote this letter hoping she would win for her "Golden Touch." She did not and that is fine. She is a winner in my heart. I love you Toya very much and appreciate your dedication to being a wonderful friend and badazz stylist.

GOT JOKES

Yeah, I will make light of anything so I will not stress. I will call myself a fat ass in a heartbeat, while others say girl you are not fat or you carry it well. Then I hit them with "Look you haven't seen me naked." I even shock people making light of MY diagnosis. I am not going to sit around as if this is the end for me. Like I said this is only the beginning. One day my close friend and I Angela Bush-Robinson went to Red Lobster to eat. I had a craving for lobster and crab legs for some time and I do not know if it was because of the commercials that continuously came across my TV screen or it was just time for a seafood binge. Well this particular day Angela and I made a few stops before eating. All day I received compliment after compliment along with a few discounts. Once we seated at our table two men at the bar kept looking our way. One finally got the nerve to walk towards our table, extend his hand with an announcement of his name. Then a message from his brother came there after, wanting to know if he could buy me a drink. I responded by letting him know I do not drink alcohol, however I could stand a nonalcoholic Strawberry Daiquiri. He returned to the bar and recited what transpired between us. His brother, who is from Atlanta, Georgia, signaled the server and placed my order for my drink, he raised his glass and smiled my way saying, enjoy. I returned my million dollar smile as appreciation for his generosity. "Damn girl! Angela says you have been getting hooked up all day long what's up with that." I said plain and simple as I admired my tall glass that held the redder than red slushy elixir which was topped off with the sweetest strawberry I had ever tasted, "Girl, you better get you a dose of that HIV." We bust out laughing. That was the best nonalcoholic drink I have ever had. What I want you to get from this is, make the best out of your situation. I dare not make fun of someone else's disease they may not feel the way I do or be able to handle the joke, but for me it is therapeutic to laugh about it just as it is putting it on paper. LOL!

WHAT ABOUT MY BABIES?

How am I going to tell them about me having this disease? I knew I would have to tell them something. They came over to the hospital everyday with the exception of one day. My oldest daughter spent that time in the group home. My youngest daughter would go straight to the lounge down the hall from my room after she would speak and kiss her mommy. Why she did not stay with me during their visit puzzled me. Mainly because at home she smothered me with attention, always rubbing my feet and telling me how beautiful I was, as she is doing now as I am typing this. My oldest was the opposite, she was not as affectionate as my youngest, but while I was in the hospital, she did not leave my side. She combed my hair, greased my scalp, put Vaseline on my chapped black lips, fluffed my pillows, even cleaned out my sink, and watered my beautiful roses Robert Thurman brought me. Thanks again Big Baby. I told my girls I had a liver infection. In all honesty I did. I continued to struggle with the thought of them finding out in the street. I did not want them to face the unknown with the truth. It was my place to let them know. Keeping it real with my girls was important to me. Therefore, late March I told the girls I had HIV. They saw the commercials; I had the talk with both of them about abstaining from sex until marriage. They participated in HIV/AIDS Prevention programs at after school; now they were face to face with it. Their first teacher, their mommy, a strong dark-skinned, big boned diva was infected with a disease that could take her away if she did not take care of herself. My oldest daughter took it the worst. She screamed and hollered to the top of her lungs and her peanut butter colored hands covered her ears as she ran down the green mile, known as my hallway to her room. I called our family meeting to talk about their feelings, she continued to rebel against conversations about it. Now my youngest seemed to take it well, however I was still curious to know what was going on inside of her little mind and heart that she was not sharing. I immediately contacted my case manager with the Metrolina AIDS Project and she referred me to Timmons & Thompson's, now Youth Network for counseling. Dr. Daphne Timmons and Keith Noland did a wonderful job in helping the girls channel aggression and feelings with whatever is bothering them. I will tell anyone I am not too proud to seek assistance when needed, especially for my mini divas. One particular day my oldest had a project to complete so I dropped her off at the library while my youngest and I grabbed a table at the McDonald's across the street for a bite to eat. When we sat down and blessed our food as we always do before eating, she says to me, "Mama, Can I ask you something", I said, "Yes, baby what it is?" "Do you have AIDS?" I said "Yes." She said, "How did you get it?" I told her from having unprotected sex. Not using a condom and being irresponsible, the same thing I tell her and her sister repeatedly. "Wait until you are married. After you complete college and establish a career having and owning your own home with whatever car you chose to have." Then she asked, "Are you going to die?" My heart has dropped at this point, as I take a deep breath and I tell her, "Baby girl we live to die, it's what you do in between that determines were your soul will rest." I felt confident in my choice of words and I guess she did to, because her last question was, "Mom", "Yes baby", I said. "Would you like some ketchup for your fries?" My oldest said to me recently as we were dusting the furniture in the living room one Saturday morning, "Mom I forget you have HIV." I tell her, "That's what they say I am not claiming anything. That's what they diagnosed me with, I believe in a miracle and so should you, now keep dusting." I thank God every chance I get I praise him through laughter, tears, and in everything I do day after day and that you should do the same. Kids are so innocent and naïve to so much and it is our duty as parents to be more responsible with ourselves, for we are their first teachers. Talk to your babies and keep it real with them. If you do not the streets will, the TV will add some more twist to the drama and the videos can set off the cannon to explode and please don't forget monkey see monkey do. Clean up your own act so they will know how to represent first for themselves in public towards others and for you. Remember you are your child's first teacher.

STARTING OVER

The thing that bothered me the most was acceptance by the opposite sex. Jermaine was faithfully by my side. At least I thought, I did not see him as much but I talked to him daily. It made me feel like he did not want any thing to do with me any more. This was not the case. I will get to that later. I got a visit from a representative from the North Carolina Health and Human Service Department. When this short Caucasian woman stepped into my living room, I felt a sincere vibe from her. I was watching Tyler Perry's Madea's Family Reunion. She was delighted about his performance. Can you believe that she sat and watched this DVD with me? I enjoyed having her around. I must say I have encountered some loving and caring people on this long journey to recovery. Her duty was to compile a list of all of my previous sex partners, so they could test them. Yeah right! I honestly felt Jermaine was the one, but test after test proved he was not. The person that is doing FED time also aced the test. I had so many partners I could not keep up with them. However, one had wanted to get with me after many attempts of getting me in bed. After turning, his attempts down numerous times, me should have kept saying NO! 10 seconds was not worth my life. Now I am not bragging it is what it is 10 seconds; I felt I had the baddest down there between my legs. After the short interaction we shared. He jumped up and shouted, "I can't do this!" I felt myself between my legs and said, "You already did!" I did not think about asking, "Do you have HIV", Use a condom, or better yet NO! This left me with this disease. I contracted this disease from a casual relationship from a person I did not have any feelings. Was it worth it Hell No! A lot of people and things are important to me my kids, my family and my new given nickname, RASBERRIROSE. I bet you all are curious in where that came from. Well Jermaine gave me this name. Initially he called me cupcake. I did not like that; because it represented softness and I was so afraid of getting hurt, I tried too hard not to let the inner mushy me unfold before his or anyone else's eyes, but it was impossible not to with him. My Grandmother name was Rosetta and he knew how much she meant to me and my last name is Roseborough, now the Rasberri was a pet name combined with the rose and there it is. Have you ever had a person to make you feel like you were in junior high all over again when his presence graced the room? That was Jermaine. He has this way of taking his hand and rubbing it across my chest and my knees would buckle when I got overexcited and would say, "Stop it." Jermaine was every thing I wanted with the exception of having another. We had a saying that we would be friends to the end like Chucky & his bride. I developed a relationship with myself thanks to him. He showed me how to spend time with myself and not depend on any man to occupy space. Something my mother told me all along, but I did not listen. He knew what I wanted and he was great at supplying all of my needs, until he left to go home. I needed him around; I wanted to be the one and only lover in his life. It did not work out that way so I settled for what I could get. No, it is not okay, but through this experience, it allowed me to become a stronger woman.

I HAVE AIDS!

Yes, you are supposed to tell anyone you come sexually involved with that you are positive. It is the law in the State of North Carolina, attempted murder is the case they can give you, or should I say the person deliberately spreading the disease. I have come across many brothers that have asked could I have a hug and thanked me for being so honest with them. Others appreciated the heads up. However, no more phone calls. I felt so much pain due to the fact I may have grown fond of the person and he gave up an opportunity of getting to know some one as special as me. My mom wanted me to let people get to know who I was not the woman that has HIV. She felt I should not engage in sexual activity with anyone who is not my husband anyway. This is something I wished I had done a long time ago. Nevertheless, I being who I was had to learn the hard way. It came to a great surprise that many wanted to continue to have relations with me. That is why I encourage everyone to get tested you have individuals who do not mind being with individuals with the disease with or without a condom, screaming we are in this together! My mind drifted and I wanted to kill myself, I had purchased a 380 from the gun store and wanted to die, I wanted to run my car in a cement barrier, take a hand full of pills to ease the pain of my heart, the rage in my mind and the secrets many known and unknown had no idea I carried within. The truth of the matter is I do not have AIDS and it will not have me, I have control of it I would tell myself, believing in His word that I am healed. Newcomers invaded my life, because of my lack of judgment of course, only wanted to sweep me off my feet as they spit no one will ever love you, you have that shit. Trying to break me down and have me feel exactly what they are saying is true. I do not think so. I do not endure pain well and I began to think logically after the indecisive ways on how to kill myself. If I run my car in the wall I may come out with a broke neck, if I shoot myself I may survive the bullet and suffer from headaches and the pills who wants their stomach pumped. The ultimate thought, it is a sin and my soul will not rest for eternal peace if I commit this act, this ungodly way of death to cease the feeling of me having AIDS!

LOVE, LIFE AND LONELINESS

As the summer of 2004 was ending my T-cells were increasing and my viral load was low which was a great thing. I continued to eat healthy foods, exercise and record my daily thoughts. My birthday was approaching in October and I wanted to have all of my friends and family near to help celebrate another year. At least that is how I felt. Therefore, I planned my own surprise birthday party with the help of two very special friends. I gave my friends my Rolodex to call everyone who had special meaning to me. Every one was asked to bring a single red rose and a select few was asked to bring a covered dish, you know you have to be careful with who is cooking what you eat. The only problem was Jermaine did not show up. He called earlier that day and told me happy birthday and that he will see me later still no Jermaine. As headlights gleamed through the window, I jumped up hoping to see his face. We danced, ate good and got drunk as hell, yep I celebrated my birthday. After the party shut down, I went into my room and cried myself to sleep, not understanding why he did me this way. We are friends to the end. I needed him there. When I woke Saturday morning, my eyes were puffy and sore. I did not call him but later I received a call from him stating that he had to be at work the following morning and that is why he did not come. I did not believe him. I received a letter in the mail later that day stating that as of 10/31/04 my Medicaid benefits would terminate for making to much unearned income, what the fuck! Some of my medications averaged to two thousand dollars for a thirty day supply each. I have HIV! What am I going to do? I cried I worried myself so until my viral load went up and I was at-risk once again. I do not have to tell you how great God is. My lovely case manager with the Metrolina AIDS Project stepped in and provided me with the support and services that I needed. Ms. Angela you are another angel I will carry in my heart forever. A blessing received, once again during the elections, politicians lifted the waiting list for the ADAP Program, which is a government funded program that allows HIV and AIDS patients to receive no to low cost prescriptions. The worst part of it all was I would lose my ID Consultant, Dr. Verville; He did not want to lose me as a patient either. We developed a relationship were I trusted and respected my caregiver. It only got better; I told you God was good. Dr. Verville's Nurse Theresa called me to let me know of another office they were merging with and I would get to see Dr. V. Ecstatic was the feeling I got. Thanking Jesus for his mercy and grace for if it were not for Him this would not be possible. I was able to sign up for a sliding fee scale at my new Doctors Office. Every thing seemed to be back on track again. At least I thought. My new Doctor was not as personal as my other Doctor was. The office it self was not inviting and some not all of the staff was not very friendly. Well after going back where I should have stayed I am back with Dr. Jessica Saxe and I will see my new ID Consultant at CMC Biddle Point Office starting July 2005. "Give it to God and let him handle it, Mama says all the time, but you have to leave it with him Vonda." I started to learn this as my tail continued to get soft. I worry so much and cry so easily since my diagnosis my mom started calling me boo bear. I was sensitive to movies, newspaper articles and news stories, tears flowed for the simple things. I think of tears flowing as a cleansing, thanks Michelle Dorsey. My God is a mighty God and he has shown me this in each day, which is why when I wake I say Thank You Jesus. He wanted me to become humble, patient, loving and caring and to be sensitive to others and their needs.

WHAT IS IT NOW?

Yeah, you guessed it. Something else was up but I could not put my hands on it, even though the feeling was there, I had my health and strength, a lot of faith and so many loved me what else could I ask for. Drop it like its Hot! Where is Jermaine? I have not seen him is what rolled off my tongue as I talked to myself, trying to figure it all out. It was the weekend of Thanksgiving, 2004 and I had not seen or heard from Jermaine since the Saturday after my birthday. "I know he isn't mad at me because of him hurting my feelings, spoiling my day", I say to myself. Having me put on a phony face at the party with folk who knew me, except for Ebony who took the 12 bottles of Andre about 20 Margaritas to the head and still knew something was not right. She offered to stay, but she was only going to go to sleep on me. Not saying the party was not appreciated, hell I set it up, just playing. Well to my surprise, I received a call that Saturday night around 7:00 p.m. As I looked at the caller ID, I saw his name appear. Excited but on the defensive I picked up the phone no longer longing for this moment. Not letting the smoothness of this brother get to me, I will leave a little bit to myself. The conversation started with why? "Why did you do me this way, I thought you and I were friends to the end? You were going to support me on this you were supposed to be there." I told him that sneaky incognito stuff was going to catch up with him. Remember to trust your gut instincts it tends to steer me in the right direction, even if it causes heartache and pain. His response was straight to the point. Jermaine said, "You are doing too much! You are letting every one know about your HIV status, putting me out on front street." He did not want to step up in the party in fear of who would know him or somebody who knew somebody that knows him. That person is messing around with the woman with that shit. Please let me tell you I do not have the shit, I have HIV. I hate to hear people say that. Far as I am concerned, it was my business to put it out there. People needed to know. It had gotten out on his ex-girlfriends job due to an email she received. Therefore, she was entitled to know for her well being. He felt as if he could not go through what he has already went through with me again. Hell I felt like I was the one who went through the storm. Not being selfish or anything, but he tested negative, thank you Jesus. "I thought we were in this together", I said, as my mind continued to ponder his next word. "You know I love you and care for you a lot, he said. This is what got me. Jermaine continued with, remember the baby I told you about last year that may be mine." I said to him, "Baby! Jermaine I don't know any thing about a baby, yes I remember a little girl you say may be yours that is up in age, but not a baby." "Yes I did." He said. "No you didn't. What baby!" I screamed. She is 10 months old. I got her name and she was born here in my city. That took me for a loop. To my surprise, I felt more pain hearing what he said to me than the Dr. telling me I was HIV positive. I experienced so much pain and hurt from that conversation all I could spit was, "How could you, How could you jeopardizes that lady and baby like that! Knowing what we went through last year." He told me this lame line. "Well I have had negative results and so did she and the baby, so I felt we were okay." I told him yeah you have negative results right now, but did you know that you can have negative results and not get a positive until many years later, it happened to me!" Before I knew it, I had done a five minute public service announcement to this irresponsible; I do not want any more kids, playa playa. "Okay so you think because your test came back negative and hers from the birth of the baby that it was okay to have unprotected sex." I told him what my mom told me a nurse over at Carolinas Medical Center told her when I had my first born, "girl be glad it's a baby and not AIDS!" "What about the partners she had unprotected sex with, what about yours? Hey! I have AIDS." Yeah the conversation got deep. We ended with me saying he could have kept that to himself. I resented him for hurting me and putting not only himself but also a woman and child at-risk. For a long time we did not communicate. I went through Christmas 2004, Martin Luther King Day passed, Valentines Day was just another day and I still had no communications with Jermaine. I text messaged him repeatedly; I left messages and still no response. One day he left a text telling me, "U has some audacity calling me immature and childish, that U R the immature and childish one, U can't handle it so I choose not to deal." He is one of the ones that gave me strength. I am going to tell you about circumstances in a book titled, "It Goes Down in Creektown", and a compilation of incidents in past relations that taught BeBe a life learning lesson. Lesson well received in order to be the head strong, determined woman that I am now. I feel journal writing, creating characters with choices and consequences, is therapeutic for my mind and me being as creative as I am allows me to put it on paper. Learn from your mistakes do not let repeat offenses do to fault of your own have you looking like a silly sally sausage head. I went through some things and I am still going through some things, However I had to realize once again, that a person takes you as far as you allow them to. Learn to love you for who you are learn to be who you need to be for His purpose, God not man or any one else. Do not make it bad for yourself. Treat yourself the way you want someone else to treat you. Again, I state the situation was part my fault. I wanted so much out of it for me with this person, and I risked my feelings as well as my health all for the sake of being in love. What I have done I cannot take it back. Someone asked if you could start over would life be different, "Hell yeah!" I would start my life from the womb and make drastic changes in the people places and things I involved myself with that were toxic to me. Well I cannot go back but I do have a second chance at life, I am still a mother, a friend, a lover, a daughter and I believe that through the grace and mercy of God I will be all right. My T-cells are 270, viral load is 800, and I am healthier than I was this time last year. The windows of blessing continue to pour for me as to have as many great opportunities thanks to the Metrolina Aids Project. My case manager Ms. Angela Headen provides me with so many services I do not know where to start. She is an angel, helping me get my medications through the ADAPE Program, free dental services through the Ryan White Title II program and primary care with my physician and specialist. I took advantage of every thing I could. I have no shame in my gain. On the anniversary of my first year living with HIV, I spent the evening at a Christmas party at the AGAPE Center, were families affected and or infected by HIV/AIDS joined together in fellowship, food and birth of our Savior Jesus Christ. I was coming to terms that some one has to do some thing to help those seeking a way out from making the same mistakes I did. Through the good times and the bad times, I press on. Through the happy times and the sad times, I pray harder. He brought me through a powerful storm.

JERMAINE

Jermaine and I are still friends. It took me a long time to get it through my thick head that we were not going to be more or less. He helps me sort out no nonsense issues. He speaks positively about achieving my goals and respecting my gangster. At times I find myself having flashbacks on the situations I endured with Jermaine, when we are on the phone and something triggers, I let him know that I am having a flashback and he says goodbye. I do not hold him accountable for my choices because it was my decision to indulge in the behaviors that I permitted myself to engage in with him. I sometimes call him he sometimes answers, he sometimes call me I may miss the call. What ever the case may be he will always hold a special place in my heart. Mainly because it was through the Jermaine experience that helped me becomes a better woman. Making decisions at what man enters my life to accepting the alone time as what it is, spending time with me.

THEIR TESTIMONY...MY BREAKTHROUGH

Let me tell you not all was that bad. I have a funny story to tell you about the day I met Fantasia Barrino. I tried to purchase some tickets to a one night stand concert Fantasia was putting having at The Big Chill's on a Thursday evening in Charlotte, NC. Well to my surprise, you could not purchase the tickets you had to win them on WPEG Power 98 FM. Without much success, I cried each time I heard someone else had won. Finally, as I lay in bed looking over at the clock hit 9:12 AM, I changed my TV channel to BET and Fantasia's "Truth Is" video was on. Something brought me to my feet and towards my radio to win some tickets. This was the day of the show so I had to win. When I turned on the radio, I heard the down south twang coming from the speaker, Fantasia was at the radio station and I immediately started snatching my rollers out and grabbing some clothes to get to the station ASAP. When I arrived, I stood in the lobby for 1 hour and 15 min waiting for Fantasia to step off the elevator. When she stepped off our eyes met as she walked my way she spoke to others who adored her presence. I waited patiently until it was my turn to express to her how much her accomplishments and music means to me. Moreover, how my family enjoyed watching American Idol just to see her advance week after week. I told her about my 2003 positive HIV diagnosis and that her CD was an inspiration to me. "Every time you sing, my favorite song This is Me, think of me", #12 on the Free Yourself Album. This song tells a story that I wish for day after day. She hugged my neck, we both shed a few tears and she told me she would keep me in her prayers and that every thing was going to be okay. No, I did not get to see her in concert but that was a far better experience. My friends tell me they are going to have to call medic when I meet Mary J. Blige. Mary you must know that you helped me through your songs to cope with the worst of times and rock to the beat during the best. I have to give Quartez Guyton all the credit for putting me up on the My Life cassette. I played that bad boy so much it popped. Your struggle was all too familiar to me and to watch you grow and mature and through your music you share with the world, the personal obstacles you overcame. You helped me in more ways than you will ever know. Thank you so much Mary I am your #1 fan. I knew one day that this I am about to tell you was going to happen. I call myself Sylvia Brown from the Montell Williams Show (Joking). I was constantly seeing special programs on Magic Johnson on ESPN and CNN. I inspired by his accomplishments and dedication to Keep the Ball Moving as Stedman Graham titled one of his books. I spoke at a church in Charlotte and told the people that I will be the female Magic. Well after the speaking engagement, a Pediatric RN over at Carolinas Medical Center, Mary Dewalt, who also treated the first infected baby at the hospital came up to me and said you are going to hear Magic speak at the Ninth Annual HIV Update at the Carolina Theater up at Duke University. I was ecstatic. I could not wait for March 21, 2005 to get here. I loaded up on the van with others from MAP and listened to Fantasia all the way there and back. Not knowing I was going to be the third person to stand with the microphone and comment on what I admired about him and what my intentions were with the fight against HIV/AIDS. He applauded me for taking my medicines as I am suppose to and encouraged me in letting my voice heard. I have a story to tell, I have a mission to complete, and it is all in his plan (God). I know in my heart that God allows me to see through experience that only a fool will make the same mistakes in repetition. Doing the right thing by myself primarily allows me to treat others as well as others treat me, with the respect, we all deserve. I still have issues to battle, my latest one was stressing over putting out this book. My friends and family knew about my situation. As I spoke, publicly many more found out. Letting the world know my story was another obstacle to battle. I took a Speakers Bureau Training with the United Way Central Carolinas, another avenue towards prosperity. Our final group assignment was to define a tough obstacle or so called failure I have had to overcome something that is important part of 'who I am.' When it was my turn to answer, I could not complete the assignment. I was at a lost for words and my adrenaline skyrocketed and the tears started to form. Through the words of Ms. Debbie Howze, Case Manager for the Metrolina Aids Project at the time, "You have a powerful testimony to share with someone who can benefit from your words", I believe in you, do not worry about what no one else is thinking you have something to say." Thanks Ms. Debbie for believing in me. With my faith in his mercy and grace, I believe (Thanks Fantasia). I am not ashamed of anything I have done. If I could take it all back, I would, well I cannot. Therefore, I take each day and live each day to the fullest surrounded by supportive, loving individuals that care. In spite of any raging storm, I know my Father in heaven would not put any more on me than I can handle. To you the reader, if you are suffering from any addiction, disease, loss of a loved one, rape, raising/being raised in a single parent home, public housing, and/or welfare, whatever your circumstance may be, TRUST IN HIM (God). He will never leave you or forsake you.

ALMOST THERE

As I sit in my yard and sip on lemon tea and type on my laptop, I wonder will anyone get any thing out of me pouring my issues out in this book. I sure am! Well if no one else did, I learned from my own mistakes. Do not beat your self up over spilled milk, but if you keep dropping the glass use a cup.

I have a large circle of friends who feel comfortable in confiding in me about issues ranging from relationships, kids that are confused and even putting outfits together. Some come to get my take on sex. Some seem to think I know everything when it comes to sex. I wish. I would not be in the predicament I am in now, which I count as a blessing to me now rather than a bad choice. One day I was taking a walk through the neighborhood and my cell phone blurted out the ring tone of All I Need by Method Man and Mary J. Blige. I answered acknowledging Destiny because her number programmed in my contact list. Destiny is not her name. I call her Destiny because the Webster's World Dictionary defines *Destiny as seemingly inevitable succession of events ones fate.* Destiny has been through it all, more than would require her own story told. On this day, Destiny says to me "Vonda, I need to talk to you." "Speak on it." I say to her. She starts to tell me about a person she met in her night class and the intimate encounter they experienced. My first question I ask anyone who calls me in reference to sleeping with someone is "did you use a condom?" The silence invading the line further let me know that they were not responsible. Secondly, "what if you got an STD, HIV or pregnant, the worse thing taking it back to your husband?" Yep! Home girl is married. She says to me, "listen! Please just hear me out." I am fair to those wanting advice. When you call on me for comfort I got your back and of course expect chastisement for being foolish, however I never end the conversation with I told you so. "I know I messed up. Destiny screams burning my ear to the level of wanting to end the call, just hear me out!" To make a long story short, no condom used and the sex was great. In the mist of the sweating and panting how good she felt, Destiny recalls the feeling she had when she closed her eyes to concentrate even more on the passion they created during their act of adultery. I am not casting any stones just proving a point. "Vonda I saw your face!" When she closed her eyes, she saw my face. Picture that. I stopped her and told her, "Then you should have stopped, you should not have engaged in an extramarital affair in the first place. Do I waste breathe when I am kicking real talk to you? You see me on top of you and him behind me. Now that your eyes are open, can you see the women he has been with unprotected? No!" She later found out that she contracted a sexually transmitted disease, not from the brother from her night class but someone else. Come on people there comes a time for us to be responsible for our feelings and actions. We can fall weak for that feeling we desire for the flesh. Do not get caught up, abstain or Rap it up! Analyzing everything that went wrong versus what went right, I concluded that I was searching high and low in all the wrong places for love. I cannot blame it on my father not being a part of my life, or the way I looked as a child. I only had to accept what I looked like was not who De Vondia was. I bet you are wondering what I am doing now. I know what I am going to do with the rest of my life, what are you going to do with yours? What my Father did not do for our family I chose not to put in this book. It did not stop me from achieving my goals. I made my share of mistakes and I learned from mines and others. I hope you do the same. Get tested and Rap it up! This is not the end; this is the beginning of whatever He (The Creator) has in store.

THE SPRING VISITOR

The saga continues, I told you that this was not the end and that putting all of my innermost thoughts and feelings on paper would continue to help me heal through all of the issues of my heart. At this point, I am still waiting on my book to grace the shelves of bookstores worldwide. Therefore, until then I count all of the days and nights to come as a reason for the prolonging of this must read memoir, because day after day things continued to happen. Back in the year 1999 mid 2000, I was dating a guy, rather having sweat drenching sex with him several times day. We had drunk more malt liquor than the law allowed and drained it during unprotected sex. Well you may wonder why I not remembered him and suspected the second person accused; remember Jermaine was the first and his test results still come back negative. Two reasons, one I forgot him, and due to the numerous encounters that scorned my Pandora's Box hell as I think about it, there is no excuse or reason. Not unless you want to say, I ran out of paper of the list of who hit. Now I apologize to no one for keeping it real and some may think I am too real but it is too many women out her out of control and need to hear the truth. For the past three years, he has come by the house to see me, around the same time of the year each time, during the month of April. In April 2004, three months after my release from the hospital I got a knock on the door one Sunday after church. I was preparing dinner and happy to see the tall brown-skinned, hazel-eyed brother on the opposite side of the threshold. He was always dressed to perfection and had the prettiest curly hair. He told me he had gotten married and was happy with children. His family did not live to far, dropped by to see them, and wanted to check on me and see how I was doing. I expressed to him about what I had been through recently and my newly diagnoses and how good God had been to me. After we talked about my health and me, he hugged me and left. I did not see or hear from him again until late April 2005 when he popped up again to see how I was doing. I did not think much of it, old friend stopping by to see how I was doing, until March 2006. This time he came five days before the month of April was to arrive. My daughter came to the bathroom door and told me a man wanted to see me. "Who is it?" I asked. She said his name, "Tell him I am coming." I had just gotten out of the shower; I slipped on some shorts and a shirt and wrapped my hair up in a towel. I went to the front door; he was walking up the driveway. He looked to be taller than usual, eyes beautiful as ever and he was much bigger than before, all in the right places. He started how good it was to see me and went with the usual, that he was here to see family and decided to stop by and check in on me. "You are still sexy." He kept saying repeatedly, and I said, "You are married." I asked about his family and he said they were fine. I reminded him of my diagnoses and how I was doing thus far in my life and you know he act as if I had not told him. He said I told him I had a stroke. "No, I did not!" I said. Then I noticed a large pebble sized tears fall from his eyes. "I am okay, do not cry." I said to him. "I can not lose anyone else." He says. I am like WOW, what in the world is going on here? "Explain this feeling to me." I encourage him to be as open as possible about his feelings. "I cannot tell you what you want to hear, I should have given you what you wanted back then." He said. "This would not have happened to you… this was not supposed to happen to you… you are a good girl… if I would have stayed with you." He babbled on and on. All of this and on top of that tears, I was in complete shock at this point. I looked deeply into his eyes, feeling one thing and asking another. "Would you have remained in my world during my recovery, hell after I told you I was positive with

AIDS? What about the 23 days I was in the hospital, preparing my food, taking my baths, lotion my body and back and forth to the doctors' appointments?" He responded with a loud, "Yes I did it for my baby's mother, she died of AIDS!" Hold up brother, I am thinking. However, my mouth saying, "When did she die?" "She passed in 2005." He said, "When was she diagnosed." I asked immediately. "She tested positive a year and a half prior to her death." He said as he began to relax and the tears became a drought on his face leaving ashy stains above his lips. "Well first off, I said, she didn't die of AIDS; she died from complications of the disease. What was wrong?" I asked. "She didn't take her medications." He said as his head dropped and began to tear up again. He started saying I cannot lose any one else again. My heart felt he wanted to tell me something and I acted on it. I said to him, "You have something to tell me, I feel it." My thoughts were damn; I had just learned two months before this that someone that I had sexual contact with had died in 2005 from complications of AIDS and now this. Remember the person at the party and the feeling I got when he walked up. I was in total shock again, with this feeling more intense. Still not ashamed for what I have done. Just know that I continue to have a story everyday of my life to share and bold enough to do something about it. Stand up people; stand up okay back to the spring visitor. I continued to grill him on my thoughts of him needing to express his feelings to me, because he was too emotional for me. He was the only person I had saw face to face affected to this degree about my diagnoses. I was able to calm my daughter down in a matter of minutes. He wanted to go to the park and talk, he wanted to go to the lake and walk, I said no to his request, "Not without your wife I want to meet your wife", I said, trying to ease some of the anxiety. So why did I allow him to stick around, you may wonder? I deserved an explanation for the excessive tears and the expressive words that showed deep concern. My mind was in whirlwind, steady trying to figure out why I saw him once a year around the same. His baby mother diagnosed in 2003, probably around the same time I was. He was probably checking on me to see if I was still alive. Spitting denial when I told him for the second time I was positive, confused I was, nevertheless I did not let it shut me down, and I still had something to do. Remember God left me here for a reason. I changed our environment to influence more dialogue between us. I hoped to get him to confess to something I felt he was willing to tell. I was truly sick and tired of the crying and needed to know what was going on with him. I was out of my element now and probably decreasing my T-cells by stressing right along with him. We decided to walk to the neighborhood store, I needed a cigarette and I had quit smoking. It was beginning to get chilly outside and I had on a light jacket, but he insisted that I wear his. "No!" I said. I hated the pity party. I disliked the way he made me feel, as if he was trying to make up for something he did to me. He placed his arm around me when guys in the neighborhood walked by or drove by. I would yell at him, "Don't do that, and keep your hands off of me." He asked, "Why do you treat me this way? All I wanted to do was comfort you." "Comfort me, your wife dude, you are married, we are just friends!" I did not want to make him upset, because I knew there was something he wanted to say to me and I did not want to disturb the conversation. From 4:30 in the afternoon until 9:30 that evening, I grilled him like a T-bone on a summer's day. As we walked back from the store towards my house, I closed my eyes and walked briskly ahead of him. I closed my eyes and asked God to be with me and humble me through this encounter. He asked me why I was walking so fast and to slow down. I slowed my pace as he told me to stop completely and that he loved me. I giggled in the inside because this whole day was a complete joke. He had the nerve to tell me that he wanted to be with me and that he would leave his wife for me. "No sweetie, please do not do that and it's not right, plus I am not in love with you. Please stay with your wife." I said to him. He stopped in the middle of the street as I continued my stride back towards home reciting, "Don't you have something to tell me?" I cannot tell you what you want to hear, I just cannot do it." He continued to say. This time it clicked, was it you I fell for the Okie doke? I felt this was going to be a hassle and did not really want to deal with it, but I needed to. We came back and sat down in the living room and I tried to make small talk. But it was so deep that my older bother JoJo who was lying in the living room floor when we arrived back at the house listened as oh boy continued to not only confess his love, but the tears showed back up along with his fear of losing someone else. My brother looked at me with wide eyes and said, "Watch that nigger; I believe he gave you that shit." I shook my head in agreement, to what he had said. I confided in my brother on how perplex I had become since his arrival. Then my brother asked me was I going to church and I replied, "Yes." "Follow your heart Sis; do you think he is the one?" Possibly, were the thoughts ravishing my mind, but hell it could be anybody? I still needed more so I took him to another area of the house, as if I stay in a mansion or something. We came to my bedroom and my direct orders were, DO NOT TOUCH ME! He began to cry again and this time I was tired of his pathetic pool of tears. I boldly asked, "Do you have HIV?" "No!" He yelled and the tears dried up faster than a mouth with peanut butter and no milk. He went on to claim he had lung cancer, the chemo was making his hair come out, and he refuses to take the pills that the doctor prescribed. I gave him a hug and told him I was sorry to hear about his diagnoses. However, my heart begged to differ. He started with the love he had for me and I headed him towards the door to say goodnight. My mind was blown and the cigarette was not strong enough, I needed a blunt to ease the tension I felt drained me from the day's drama. I ended up going to sleep instead.

PAPER & PAIN

I remember as if it was yesterday, my car was in the shop needing a starter and my account drained after her minor surgery. I sat as I was pondered the rest of the month and my desire for a cigarette. I looked out the window and reminded by the open space in my driveway that my car was in the shop and again another sign to be still and listen. No, I had to take a walk to the corner store to buy a lucy; a lucy is a single cigarette. This particular day was a bad day anyway, my car was in the shop, my bank account was going to be zero and my emotions were haywire. I could not fight the feeling I was having and for some reason I did not want to. I wanted to drown in my own pity. What was happening to the strong DeVondia that needed no one to talk to about her problems, what was happening to the DeVondia that consistently kept God in her prayers and asked for forgiveness when she did wrong? Why did I feel the world was tumbling down on me with out enough of rope to hang myself? I am living with AIDS, sick to my stomach and lonely as I ever been before. The cigarettes are my only way to ease the pressure since my body rejects the weed I so wanted to ease the issues of my heart. I inhaled the stale taste of about three lucies, I decided to call Tipp and talk to her on the phone for a little while. My stomach began to ache after I devoured a tasty Tyson's chicken potpie. I stood up and a sudden dizziness announced its presence. I suddenly flashed back to my 2003 fainting spells. I increased my pace towards my bedroom, because I told yawl my hallway is the green mile, it seems like forever to get to the back of the house. I made it safely to my bed, only to see the big round eyes of my youngest daughter filled with worry as she sees the discomfort in my face. I let her know I am lying down for a while and all she wanted to know is was I all right. I let her know I did not feel well as I laid down my heart began to beat faster and out of control. I could hear the thumping repeat with a thrust so powerful that all I could do is cry out to God for peace and release the fear that I was experiencing. My feet began to get cold and the tips of hands began to feel the same. The same feeling I had when I smoked that last blunt. See God got my attention off blunts and I was disobedient and had to learn another lesson for my full attention off cigarettes to on Him. I started going to the bathroom to do the number two, real talk I thought I was dying. You know they say you have that last bowel movement before you pass on. My brain was moving around in my head, I could feel the moisture surrounding it moving against my skull. The next day was For Sista's Only, I did not want to miss the largest event of the spring in Charlotte, authors, poets, national, and local artist come together for a day of family fun. How can I enjoy this yearly ritual with my girls if I am stuck in the hospital again, and I had bought the tickets already? Tipp, the only person besides my mother I could call at anytime and answer the phone when in need. I had no car, no clue to what was going on with me and I needed to go to the hospital ASAP. She was there in a hop, skip and a jump to escort me ghetto style to the Carolinas Medical Center. Tears began to stream down my face and my emotions where filled with fear. Not knowing whether I admitted to the hospital was the thought that bombarded my mind. I did not want to let my kids down. They looked forward to this event every year. I spent $60.00 on tickets and I needed to get them there no matter what, hell I went to the pawnshop to do that. The nurse came over and asked Tipp to wheel me over to check my vitals. My blood pressure was 135 over 77, my temperature was normal and he wanted me to calm down and breathe clearly. A RN asked me the symptoms I was having and they sent me back to be looked over by a doctor. I wheeled back by my faithful friend Tipp and the male nurse that made the ride comforting told me how my hair was like his newborn baby. He whips out a picture and this beautiful baby has a Mohawk. My stylist had put a head turner in my head and I told him he has the coolest baby in Charlotte. He had the perfect wheel side manners, as nervous as I was he made me feel a lot better. However, the anxious feeling, and the cold and hot fingertips and toes continued. Our Father who art in Heaven, I continued to say this repeatedly. I wanted every thing to be okay. I did not want to be at the hospital nor did I want to be a resident for an extended period again. The doctor was quick to come in and look me over. She immediately ruled out the possibility of a stroke or heart attack. Anxiety was an issue and an hour and a half later waiting on lab work, low potassium caused my unexplained weakness and dizzy like spells. The doctor gave me two potassium pills and a prescription for four more along with a list of foods I had been neglecting was now a priority. If you do not do it the Bibleway, trust and believe God will do it His way to get your attention. After that night, no more cigarettes, no more beer and blunts were long gone. To this day, I cannot stand the smell of smoke and some chemicals trigger anxiety attacks, but Jesus can bring me through. I pray through the attacks and no longer submit my liver going through any unnecessary toxicity than it needs.

Listen to God, listen you can hear!

TRIPPING OFF OF PAIN

I have my good days and my bad days, and Lord knows my good days out weigh my bad. Let me take you inside my heart and mind during the month of April in the year 2006. I was tired of feeling helpless and for the first four days of the month, I was not at my best. I am still single, I am still a mother, and I still have AIDS! As I looked in the mirror, I shook my head and said to me, "How could you do this shit Vonda? Why did you have to mess your life up like this? I cannot believe this!" as I walked through the door one evening carrying a Wal-Mart bag, shaking my head in disbelief, "DAMN! I got AIDS!" The burst of energy that I had a few weeks ago now filled with tears and frustration and even depression. I did not want to live and the only people that kept me sane were my children. My fake smile had changed to a face flooded with tears. Tears lined my lips, my heart ached for some one to love me and accept me for who I was, and not because they felt sorry for a beautiful dark-skinned sister with big lips. I will explain that a little later. I was so scared that I was going to die, especially after that last episode at the hospital. The relationships I conveniently caught my self up in were a waste of time and energy and even scarred my reputation, but you live and you learn. I will not waste my time going through familiar situations that I have already allowed myself to learn from, cause as I said only a fool makes the same mistakes twice. However, I have to elaborate on a few, I met a young man at a local mall and he was mesmerized by my big brown legs and my sexy eyes, let him tell it. As I tell the young women I speak to, you do not have to let these brothers come at you telling you how beautiful your eyes are and how sweet you smell, if you know that you know you do not need confirmation. Say thank you and keep it moving because we know the lame lines they use to get you. My mother felt that I should let men get to know me for who I was and not let HIV define me. My point was not everyone is on that level to accept the language I speak when I say that after two or more dates I have HIV. Just because we shook hands goodnight and kissed a couple of times an ignorant person will hurt you behind his or her lack of knowledge on the disease and think he is infected through casual contact. Therefore, I keep it real from the jump, so no emotional attachment gained and it is easy to keep it moving if they are not interested.

Well dude and I were talking for a couple of days and our last conversation went like this. "Girl you are going to make me bite you." I started to giggle because I knew he was joking, but at the same time, I expressed to him that he could not go around biting on people. He said to me, "you have a disease or something." I am in total shock; "dude did we not have this conversation in the mall when we first met, I told you I was positive and that I was an advocate for HIV/AIDS, a soon to be published author and motivational speaker." "No hell you didn't, I can not FUCK WITH YOU!" Ouch! That hurt. All I could say was okay it was nice talking to you and that was that. After that conversation, I felt a little down, but I came to realize that only I can make me feel up or down about the situation and I let that circumstance pump up my self worth. I started to love me, bump what they say I speak on it I do not claim this I am going to bounce back. I did, "what do not kill you can only make you stronger", my favorite line in Fantasia's song "This is Me". It was his lost in not getting to know the woman he had the privilege of knowing. No one is worthy of my love and affection right now, I needed to wait on God, but he was taking to long, continuing to settle for less all for the sake of love. The Bible says, He is a jealous God and again I was giving my time and dedication to someone instead of keeping my heart and mind on the Lord. A met a person that was 7 feet tall, handsome and very intelligent, but there was one problem, he stood up one day and I looked up from the TV that had the all star basketball game playing and I noticed darkness in his mouth were teeth should have been. He had taken his dentures out and did not enlighten me on that. This was an instant turn off and he did not understand how I flipped on him because of his lack of teeth, but he argued his fight that he gave me a chance with having a positive diagnoses. First, I kept it real and I let him know what the deal was with me. You should have given me the same by letting me know you remove your teeth and put them in your pocket. I know you may think you are so cruel and who are you to judge. Well I know what I prayed for and that is that. After that faded away I met another young man dark handsome and full of energy, too much energy always wanting to go and do things he could not afford to do for me or himself, but he was good company until his happiness turned into disrespect and massive anger. I had to let him go too only to be harassed on who could and could not come to MY house. So much went on with the particular person I decided not to revisit the mess for the sake of unwanted drama. Pray every night for the man that is in the will of God, I cannot and wish no woman to settle for a man just because he is a man. A man is to lead and be the head, stop letting these brothers move in on you and sleeping around not punching time clocks and when they do, they are to busy getting fly for someone else. Being easy means to me having patience, patience allows time to heal all wounds, for minds to mature and for needed strength to conquer and develop into the person God is preparing you. Think about that!

COME BACK MY CHILD

I backslid into the world again, I never said I was perfect. Just trying to walk right, talk right, and just get right. I stopped going to church and felt that TD Jakes and a little Juanita Bynum would be sufficient, not. I sat faithfully in front of the TV watching sermon after sermon and taking notes, shouting around the house, having my own praise and worship service. However, the fellowship was missing something. You know what the Bible says "When two or more touch and agree." I felt my life was tilting in another direction and reasons why I left the previous church were the needing for eagles in my circle. Now I am not criticizing the individuals in the congregation, but we all can stand to be around people that have more, know more so we can grow in our purpose that God has for us. I an intelligent woman felt there were no challenges and no room for growth. I love the pastor and his wife dearly, but God placed them in my life for that point and time and I had to move on. Nevertheless my move was back on blunts and smoking cigarettes, and drinking Bud Lights. In the midst of my sorrow and wanting to change and get out of the mess I saw myself getting back into, I started my hunt for a new church family. I found one but it was not what I was looking for. You will know the feeling when the church is right for you and your family. A friend asked me to speak at her church one day and I agreed. I sat out in the congregation as a visitor not a person that was going to get up, speak out on HIV/AIDS, and tell a personal testament. As the pastor said that, a guest speaker was here to speak out on a topic that is ravishing our community. The heads in the congregation started turning trying to see who that person was. I sat as a visitor, which I was but I find it very interesting to see the response people have and the looks on their faces when you address this topic. One young woman asked me if I knew who the speaker was; I smiled and said I am. She shook my hand and welcomed me. To the right of me a young woman was voicing how good Magic Johnson looked and that he cured of HIV. I smiled as I mesmerized by the thoughts of others and the lack of knowledge many had on the topic. As my dear friend introduced me, heads are eager to see whom this woman with this disease is to pounce up from her seat. She announced my name; I got up from the midst of the crowd, as the woman beside me looked startled that it was I about to speak truth to the thoughts and feelings many might have had about this edgy topic. What does it look like, what size is it suppose to be, it does not discriminate and I made clear first of what I heard the women say and what I heard Magic say about his diagnoses. He did not have the magic potion and because he has the money, he did not go out and buy special medicine. He takes the same medicine those that live with the disease takes. I found myself at home after I had spoke and felt only one limp hand shake, but he gave me his hand that is all that matters. I came back the following week after an invite for family and friends day and kept coming back. The sound of the drums reached inner roots, the tambourines reminded me of the old down south church my mother attended in South Carolina. The organ accompanied by four beautiful psalmist ushered in the presence of the Lord and I felt the spirit within, begging me to come back home. The pastor preached a word that understood my mind, body and soul to make the decision to bring my children on the next Sunday. But I kept smoking the blunts, I felt I had to have them, they made me feel good and I behind a good blunt a Newport to boost the high, I drunk a Bud Light or two and was set for a good football game or what ever the boys in the hood cared to watch that evening. Until one evening a friend guy of mines I was kicking it with on the down low, you know one that you do not want anybody to know about was smoking a blunt and the smoke was thick in the air. Only because it was about four blunts rotating between three people. Smoking like crazy, then all of a sudden I started to feel weird like. My head was throbbing and I felt as if my brain was moving around again inside of my head. My feet began to feel cold along with the tips of my fingers. I found myself hot all over and my body temperature shifting from cold to hot and my mind turning in leaps and bounds trying to figure out my condition. My best friend Tipp came, cleared the house, announced NO MORE SMOKING, and made everyone leave the premises. I told her to throw out every cigarette in the newly purchased Newport pack. She teased me as she asked are you sure for each cigarette she pulled from the pack. Yes, please no more, I do not want anymore. I asked her if she had ever felt that way and I remembered the feeling my sister had when she had anxiety attacks and figured that this was on me too. God was calling for His child to come back but I was not listening. As I said before my mother use to say, a hard head makes a soft you know what. I reduced the packs of cigarettes to getting lucies again. My car broke down at my mother's house. I bet you are thinking Girl that Cadillac has the most problems, and you right. However, God has allowed me to fix it every time without needing help from anybody to pay to fix it. The signs are there when God is calling for His children and I knew what they were. When you ignore the signs things happen to you out of your control and I knew being without my car would allow me to sit down and listen. Nevertheless, a hard head always makes a soft you know what, because this time I took another ride.

GIVE THEM FEVER MJB

I was ready for the Mary J. Blige concert at Verizon Amphi-theater, July 16, 2006. I went to church and I was not feeling too good, I was hiding it, at least I thought I was. My first lady told my mother I felt a little warm when she hugged me, she told me too, but I ignored it. I came home to take a nap and got myself together for the evening show. Tipp my friend is so awesome, she paid for the tickets and she told me I had better not act as if I was not going. Who me, miss a Mary J. concert? No! I do not think so. We go out to the outdoor theater and had some great seats, and I stayed on my feet through the entire concert, singing each song word for word. You can tell the ones that just jumped on the Mary band-wagon, because they were either too young to know the songs from the 411 album or they just wanted to go just to say they went. Now a true fan knows the lyrics and can tell from the intro what song she is getting ready to perform. I truly had a wonderful time, got a t-shirt and an autograph picture from one of the vendors. On the way home, I sung her lyrics and felt fantastic, until the next morning. My morning was not a good one at all. I was hot all over and I wanted to sleep. My stomach was swollen and sore on my right side. I knew something was wrong my friend guy came through and I went and got breakfast from Burger King. That is unlike me because I usually cook for him. Well I slapped breakfast on a paper plate; I lay down and was not much company to him. This went on all day, lounging and feeling sluggish all over and hot. Around 2:00 in the morning I took my temperature, which I had done throughout the day, but my concern grew more, my temperature was 103 degrees. I called my mother around 3:00 AM, she came over and got my youngest daughter and me, and we proceeded over to the hospital. All types of test were ran while I was in the emergency room, indeed there was some concern because I had a high temperature, however my spirits were bountiful and the doctors were extra nice. Well I ended up having to stay, the first time since the last time I admitted into the hospital. I began to worry and did not want to be there no longer, than I needed to. Things change when you no longer have private insurance and you are a Medicare recipient. I was rolled on the stretcher to my room and when I got inside I noticed a another bed, the doctor downstairs said she would try to get me a room by myself, even though my insurance covered a semi-private room. I did not want to share a room with no one. After I settled and met my new roommate, Mrs. Maria Mosquito a short woman with a lot of spunk from Portugal. This woman made my stay an enjoyable one, including my guest. She was in for issues with her back and I learned I had an infection on my liver that had attacked my gallbladder, which caused the discomfort in my belly and fever. I was immediately placed on antibiotics and potassium dripped from the IV. I could not do anything but lay there and pray that everything would be all right. The stylist from MasterKuts came by Toya & Barbara, Myra Foster; Editor and Chief of The Showcase Magazine came with a special treat. A comedian by the name of "Smokey" was performing at the Comedy Zone that evening and he had us cracking up, including Maria. I am laughing like crazy, as I type this remembering him and Maria have a ball. She said she wanted to Smokey to come to her house and that she liked my friends that came by, they were all so nice. Her family was the sweetest you will ever meet, she had her husband bring me fruit and crackers for our late night snack. We were watching the news and I flipped the channel to WBTV 3, and saw Magic Johnson, he was making a special appearance in Charlotte on Friday at his grand opening of Starbucks on Wilkinson Blvd. I began to cry, I needed to talk to him and let him see how much progress I had made since our first encounter at Duke University. There was no way I was going to make it. My mother brighten up my day by coming into the room with a over side black baby doll, that I named Cookie, she had on a purple dress and reminded me of Raggedy Ann with out the freckles and with dark skin. Even though released from the hospital that Thursday, I could not make it. However, you cannot keep a good woman down, I did not go but I had the privilege of being the cover model for 2005, Voices Magazine, Editor and Chief, Rita Adams. I called my faithful friend Tipp to get the book and letter I had typed up and she delivered it to the store manager. I sent him a copy as well along with a letter explaining my cause. Well by the grace of God, I did not need my gallbladder removed, my liver enzymes was high which caused my liver to swell, because of the level of toxicity of the medications I had been using over a three year period. This was indeed affecting my liver, which made my gallbladder look swollen. "No need to fix nothing that is not broke", said my specialist, I had to stay away from greasy foods and placed on a low fat diet with specific instructions to keep my gallbladder healthy. I was released from the taken my HIV medications for four months, to give my liver a break. This was fine with me, because by this time my faith was on only one, my heavenly Father. Everything happens for a reason, slowing you down only prepares you for what the Father is readying you.

FLYING TO HOLLYWOOD OR GROWING CLOSER TO GOD?

Remember when I said I wanted to take that plane trip with that special someone to Jamaica, ha! You better let God steer and you follow. Now I also expressed my fear of heights. Prayer changes everything. See September 2005, I was sponsored to go to the United States Conference on AIDS in Hollywood, Florida, and yes I flew on US Air with no problems. I stayed in the Westin Resort & Spa. I was like a kid in a candy store seeing all of the seasoned advocates from across the world come together, get rejuvenated and enhance their skills to serve the people living with HIV/AIDS. Magic Johnson, Phil Wilson of the Black AIDS Institute, Sheryl Lee-Ralph and her One Woman Show, Sometimes I Cry, and Jane Fowler, just to name a few. So many more that we could not continue to name the phenomenal people that advocate for others and me in and out of the United States. I was overwhelmed with knowledge and found new friends to call on when I needed assistance to make a better difference in my community. The beach was the perfect place to communicate with God. Sitting out on the beach with Ms. Faye, we were in separate worlds as we meditated and absorbed the beauty God has created for us to enjoy. I thanked him for the opportunity to be were I was at that moment, tears formed in my eyes to be in a state of peace with no cares or worries. To listen to God through the waves and the brisk wind that made the hairs stands on my arms. A moment in time I will never forget. I realized that God stretched me and took me out of my normal habitat and allowed me to broaden my horizon by demanding a sacrifice out of me to meet a kingdom need. Growing in the field of HIV/AIDS so that I can help others living with HIV/AIDS to seek Him and in turn reach someone else to come back home.

I TRIED TO PRESERVE MY SEXY

You seen the commercial stars talking about the blemishes and the acne taking over their faces, well I had a serious acne problem the month before my 35th birthday. I had not gotten the jet lag off me good and my face started breaking out as if I was reaching puberty all over again. I tried everything that said it could do the job. I went to a friend and she told me she had that stuff Puffy was talking about, "preserving his sexy." I neglected to read that the content in one of the stages contained sulfur. I am allergic to sulfur! My eyelids got irritated. When I went to pee, it burned. I went to the emergency room four times to be given, pain medicine, a steroid to help with the swelling and sent back home for the sulfur to continue its burning destruction through my body. My mouth became sore inside and out and it was even difficult to walk. Walking on soft carpet felt as if I was stepping on hot nails. To wring out my face cloth to wash my face was excruciating, my hands felt as if they were tingling with heat even with cold water on them. October 8, 2007 ole faithful Tipp was my way to the emergency room, ON MY BIRTHDAY. I again admitted and there I stayed for the next 15 days. The sulfur had burned me from my head to my toes. I could not walk or eat. I had blisters on the inside of my mouth that had me sipping on Ensure for daily nutrition, because it was very painful to eat, even pureed food. A large black scab covered my lips; it looked like chunks of crusty black sores on top of each other. The color of my lips had turned pink under the scab, because I had burned severely. I could not open my mouth but for so far, big enough for a straw to go in it for the liquids I had to keep flowing inside. I was in so much pain the doctors' administered morphine to ease the severe discomfort I felt, which a relief for a few hours. Every situation has a purpose even pain. I learned after a biopsy of the black spotty rash that invaded my body, the cultures taken from my vagina and the lining of my gum that everything was okay, No infections. The cause was a very rare case of Steven Johnson Syndrome. The only thing that did not occur during this ordeal was my esophagus did not close up, which my doctor said I was lucky. The prednisone given to me contained steroids could have been dangerous for me also. Self-advocacy led me repeatedly to the emergency room. I was in the hospital again, this time on my birthday. On my back the only way, I could lay looking up falling in love with Jesus Holding on to His hand. Through the tears, I praised Him, I thanked Him, and I called His name as the pain wreaked my body as I am seeking His presence to keep me sane. Remember now I was off my HIV antiviral medications because of my liver. Scheduled to go back on my medications that week, however the extra other stuff dripping from the IV and shot in my arm kept me off for a little while longer. It was nice to see familiar faces, my ID Consultant Dr. David Wenrib came by to examine me, and my primary physician came by to check on me as well. I remember Dr. Saxe saying, "DeVondia you have been through so much, you are going to be just fine." It is a blessing to have awesome care team providers, who cares genuinely. Many of my church members called, but one phone call will forever stick with me, my Pastor said, "I don't know what you are doing but, something is getting ready to happen to you that why the enemy is attacking you." I knew I was doing right and trying to be a better person, but I could not figure out why I had to lay down again. Granted I did not read the ingredients in the facemask, it was deeper than that for me. Satan indeed has a plan and he planned on stealing my joy, shutting my mouth and hushing my testimony. All of that and my experiences combined only strengthen my boldness to speak up and speak out on the victory I have won. Pain can be difficult, but pain has a purpose. My pain has driven me to my destiny. From me to you pray to God and ask Him for what you want and you shall receive, I did and more pain came for what I asked for. You have to remember, God's timing is more powerful than your things to do. He can arrest you at anytime. He is God and He has the power to make things happen all because of you to glorify Him.

THE NEXT LEVEL

I received phone calls form my case manager Angela Headen, friends Chelsea Gulden and Grant Administrator; Faye Marshall of the Metrolina AIDS Project checking to see if I was still in the hospital and when was I getting out. Why, the producers of the Oprah Winfrey Show had called and needed women that fell under certain categories to be on the 25th Anniversary of HIV/AIDS show, you know the one with Magic Johnson and his pretty wife and teeth were on. There I lay with large pebble sized tears streaming from my ducts wondering why me? Ms. Faye comforted me a little and told me if she had known I would take it like that, she would not have called. This was the worst thing that could have happened to me, you all know what happens to an individual that gets to sit on the set of the Oprah Winfrey Show. Whether it is her favorite things, a traumatic experience or her book club pick, big things happen for the unheard and the unseen. I called my mother and she told me it will be another time and when it is you will get to do what God intended for your time to be. It sounded good, but the tears kept coming and my heart was heavy. A friend of mine was able to go and she and I talked about the experience she had in Chicago, I looked out the window and a song came on the gospel station that confirmed it was not my time. I immediately encouraged myself by saying I needed the entire show and what God has for me is for me. Do not dwell on my purpose, I told myself, remember DeVondia all things done is for the glory of the Lord and remove self out of His doings, God knows what you are doing and the heart is what He looks at, not your appearance on any talk show. You remember in the beginning how I talked about no certificate or award needed to tell me how special you were, God is my source and I trust Him. A quote that leaves you thinking like it did me, "Do not follow where the path may lead. Go instead where there is no path and leave a trail." – Muriel Strode

PLEASE DO NOT LOOK AT ME!

I released from the hospital three days before the Oprah Show aired the HIV/AIDS segment, torn to pieces all over again about my inopportunity on her show. I set my DVR to record the show so that I would not miss it, in case I was sleeping and called everyone and asked him or her to look at the show. I was happy to see women like me represent themselves in a manner that inspired me to continue my fight, no shame and how dignified they looked with no worries of the backlash they may have received for their compelling testimonies. I was a tad bit weak; I lost a total of 40 pounds while I was in the hospital. I was determined to keep it off and workout to strengthen up and tone it all up. I still could not eat as much as I wanted to, but I tried. I had my mother open a can of tomatoes sautéed in garlic and onions and some water to see how I would do, it burned so bad that I neglected food with spices for a minute. I lay around a lot and slept on my back, which were sometimes uncomfortable. If I lay on my side, I risked my lips touching the pillow and the pillow slip sticking to my mouth, which caused the scab to pull from my lip and bleed like a faucet. Not to mention the pain would be terrifying to deal with. I noticed my hair falling out and the thick tresses that cover my crown and glory was diminishing before my eyes. I thinned out like a corpse loosing his last remaining strands of hair. I cried and kept my head in a scarf afraid of the stares I would get. The allergic reaction, had nothing to do with my diagnoses, it actually helped me notice that I was allergic to sulfur, but if you do not read the contents of things you are using you can end up like me, not wanting anybody to look at you. I believe I scared a lot of people by the way I looked and some even my brother thought it had to do with the AIDS diagnoses, well if it is going to scare you to be more careful then so be it. However, it is important for me to give out accurate information and I had to let people know that it was not the case. I came to realize during a point that the healing process was going to be a long one. I was in the house for three weeks, I finally came out on the porch for air but I had a mask on to prevent infection but to most definitely hide my face from the world. The scab began to dry up and go away slowly but surely, it needed to, it was already the end of October and World AIDS was approaching and I was a guest speaker at several events during the week. I had a doctor's appointment and lab work confirmed the next week my T-cell count was in the 80's and the viral load was high in my body. I knew who God was and I put back on new medication that the pharmacist repeatedly stated, "Take this every day!" I had my stylist to put weave in my hair, the big curly hair that reminded me of something Oprah wore. It looked good and I wore it well, well I wear all hairstyles well. I am told I have the face for them all. I was able to go out and find me some size 9/10 clothes; because I had lost so much weight, I could not wear the 14-16 that lined my closet. I found a black dress that fitted my new shape to the T and made me feel like a woman all over again, really for the first time. My hair was beautiful, my lips had cleared up and my Estee Lauder makeup hid the blemishes that scarred my face from the burns. I was ready for the world, but was the world ready for me?

TOO MANY SUNDAY'S OUT OF CHURCH

I was so ready to go back to church and missed the fellowship with my church family. However, I was fearful of the stigma I may receive once I came back. That was not the case, of course, I had those that looked at me extra long, but it was okay I probably would have done the same thing. I needed to hear a word from the man of God so that I would get my spiritual needs back in order. I was tired of feeling robbed of favor and blessings. I was selfish for feeling this way and knew it, but I waddled in my own self-pity just because I could. The longer I stayed away the more frustrated I became. I went to church the first weekend in November and cars dressed the parking lot but the doors to the sanctuary locked. I remembered after talking to Ms. Faye that my church family had gone to Wilmington, NC for an annual service my pastor preached at every year. Ms. Faye invited my girls and me to eat breakfast with her family. Still needing a word and wanting to sing the praises of his name among others, I waited for next week to come.

When next Sunday came, I adorned with hugs and welcome back from the lovely people of New Covenant Bibleway Church. I felt the need to testify after one of the Elders called my name out, saying "Sister Roseborough" I do not remember the rest, all I know he had repeated my name cause I did not hear him the first time from talking to someone else. I began to shout and praise the Lord, because I knew what He had done for me. I requested to hear 'I'm Still Holding On', but they were taking to long and I began singing it myself. The microphone made its way down the aisle in one of the Praise & Worship leaders hand and given to I and I began to sing what I could remember with the help of the congregation. I was compelled to stand in front of the church and sing my song. "I did not know you could sing," so many said to me. There is a lot you do not know about me I am thinking to myself. I hid behind the gifts God had blessed me with and soon confided in others that singing was a part of my life since third grade. The Holy Ghost filled my spirit and I praised Him for keeping me, allowing me to hold on to His hand!

BY HIS STRIPES

New Years Eve I decided that I was going to bring the New Year in church. This was the first time I actually had done so. I went off to church and the word was amazing. At the nearness to midnight, we began to pray and there we were reverencing God for another year, thanking Him for His mercy and grace. After prayer, we hugged one another and said Happy New Year to our family and friends. Something was eating at me in the inside a temptation like no other. One that I figured would go away, however it lingered around and I will stop there because the temptation in this flesh over weighed my ability to accept the blessing I received from God. I battled in the inside of my mind and my heart about this agony of a temptation that controlled my every thought and feeling in my body. It bombarded everything or should I say him. Yes, an emotion sung attraction to the opposite sex, the opposite sex, a committed man. Arose was the questions how, why and why me? I did not need this on me, was this test, a test of the emergency broadcast system? I could not believe what I was thinking and how I was feeling for this man and I needed it to stop. I do not want to elaborate too much, because there is another book to follow based on temptations of the flesh, titled Baptized in Warm Milk. We all have them, but what we do with them is the question. I had signed up for a Love & Forgiveness workshop at WTVI's Public Television and it helped me get deep into my innermost thoughts and feelings about those that had done or was getting on my nerves. I had long learned to forgive, but it was important for me to continue to keep this new attitude. Taking this class allowed me to interact with a diverse group of people that helped me through positive communication how to love all over again. I lay in the bed one morning, tossing and turning about to loose my mind, because I was aggravated with myself. Tore up in the inside cursing myself for messing up my life and probably not ever finding love, true love. The devil knows how strong I am someone told me one day and I shook it off, opened up the local newspaper, and saw the advertisement for the Love & Forgiveness workshop. Once I asked God to forgive me I knew it was done. It was hard to forgive myself and I meant that, therefore the sessions allowed me to communicate with me, be still and listen to Him as I picked up the phone and called the number and signed up for the free workshop. Relieved and revived after each session, I still had no one of the opposite to say I love you to, to wake up next to, to communicate my cares and wants. The test began to grow stronger and stronger. The temptations of the flesh took my life on a world wind; it controlled my mind, my walk, and even my dress. Armored with the wrong gear I could not receive the word that God had for me. Something better is in store my child he kept saying to me, just wait. Being obedient is hard when you are lonely, but obedience is better than sacrifice. I desired the need to have someone to share my thoughts with, my good news with and to wake up next to each morning to say, good morning sweetheart. January 10, 2007 I received a phone call from my pharmacist, Penny. Remember, when I go to the doctor, I see a primary care doctor and a specialist, which is an Infectious Disease Doctor. When I see my ID Doctor, he has Penny the pharmacist to come in and talk to me about my medications, the effects and the affects of the drugs. She specializes in the HIV/AIDS Medications; I say HIV meds is her expertise but compassionate is who she truly is. When she called me on that afternoon, she asked me if I was doing okay and I told her yes, lying. Calmly she said, "Well we have your lab work back and your counts great compared to what you have gone through and off the medications for three months. The medications are doing great; Ziagen, Sustiva and Kaletra have your counts looking great. Your T-cell is 350 and the virus is unde-tected." I was transparent, It went through me as if someone had said to me, strawberry or grape kool-AID? I heard it but I did not hear it, I wanted to confide in someone about my wicked issues of the heart so that it would pass me by. So that I could release the pressure that desired negative attention, I needed a TRUE WOMAN of God to mentor me. What scriptures do I read, what prayer do I pray, when will my peace arrive? That Wednesday afternoon I sat and said nothing to no one, until the phone rung and it was Ms. Faye. I told her what was just told to me and she was ecstatic. Not I, selfish and confusion had taken over my body. I called my mother with the great news and she began to praise Him, thanking Him. I, still numb as if nothing miraculous had happened to me. I let a week pass me by and not share it with many of my friends or even call my Aunt Genny. The following Sunday at church after the Praise & Worship team finished and the offering was taken up, I was filled with the Holy Spirit and I felt a chill submerge my temple and my mouth flew open and I started to say, "Family, I have something to say. I have been holding this in for a week and I must tell you last week I got a phone call and I let the enemy steal my joy. The virus is undetected in my body; by His stripes, I am HEALED! I remember my Bishop shouting out I was a miracle and the entire church was on fire, shouting and praising God for His blessing. My body jerked and tears flowed uncontrollably while I jumped and repeatedly thanked Him. My friend Tavonia came up to me after our praise party to see if the carpet was still were I stomped and stepped for joy. Bishop did not preach he made a clear statement that, "God was still in charge and in the healing business and if you did not rejoice in someone else's miracle, woo!" A mother came up to me and hugged me as she whispered in my ear, "You gave me strength and because of your healing I believe that my son will be to." If I had continued to be selfish and not testify the goodness of His promise, I would not have made a difference in someone that was weary and depressed. By testifying, you glorify His name and help someone else break through his or her go through.

DOWN BY THE RIVERSIDE

I had never been baptized and I felt I was ready to leave what challenged me in the water and once I emerged, I would be free. Free from depression, free from temptation, free from the stresses that had me bound. Of course, I knew that new issues would emerge and was sure that my mind was strong and all I needed was to be more in control of what I was thinking and by attending, Bible Study, Sunday school and studying the word was going to help me have a better relationship with my Father. All true, but that is when the enemy comes full throttle after God's Chosen One. As I walked up the stairs towards the baptismal pool, I prayed my soul to get right, for my walk and talk to be more like His and less of me. I prayed also that I would keep my eyes tight enough that I would not get my contacts and my hair wet. I dressed in all white and wrapped in a sheet, a pure white sheet draped my body and dressed on my head was a towel that tucked tightly to prevent leakage on my two bundles of wet & wavy. I walked slowly as the two Elders stood firmly in the water as the congregation looked on and sung hymns. They became quiet as one of the Elders began to pray, down I went without fear, initially I was afraid the men would not be able to hold me up, I am a big girl. I came up full and cleansed, shaking from the immediate chill that cooled my body. As I stepped up and out of the pool, I was cleansed and new, shouting thank you. As I got dressed in my clothes, anything that could go wrong started with me sooner than I anticipated. My stockings caught a severe ruin which left me without them sitting on the front row having to be covered by the delicate blue material for anyone that wears a skirt or dress with peek-a-boo that may be sitting in or around the front of the church. Service was full of joy and I was mindful of the new me that needed to get it and keep it right with God. My name called on February 11, 2007 as I presented with my official baptismal certificate. Come Unto Me it read and I did.

MOVE, GET OUT OF MY WAY!

I was sick and tired of dealing with people that were phony, jealous and stagnant. Sometimes you have to eliminate people from your life that are in the way. I did that through prayer and I did not look back. I asked God in prayer for wisdom, strength and discernment. It was so important for me to go to God first and allow Him to make His presence felt in everything I do, even the people that were there for the long haul had to get out the way. I love each one, because they all were there for a reason for that particular season. It was not an easy thing to do, but without the guidance of my Father in Heaven, I would still go through unnecessary drama with people. Unfortunately, a few did not make it another year, if I knew it was going to be that easy I would have done it a long time ago. Life is much better when I surround myself around a drama free environment that does not have to be right and know it all, all the time. Being comfortable around opinionated individuals that respect your mind and not feeling bombarded by those that think they are always right and the world revolves around them. I just thank God that I allowed me to remove myself out of the picking and choosing and let Him do His thing.

WHAT IS IT REALLY LIKE

I made up in my mind that I would not sugar coat anything and I will keep my promise. I hate me right now, I am pissed and I feel like giving up. I know I am not supposed to question you Dear Lord, but why must I feel this way. Money is tight; the kids need things and wanting things, I cannot afford. They should not suffer for my wrong doings. Nevertheless, I will sacrifice for my babies. I went to the mailbox Dear Father and I denied once again for food stamps, this would help a lot, you have people getting assistance with full-time jobs and smoking dope and here I am doing the right things and being honest with the paperwork requesting information for benefits. I get no child support to help me with the girls and my eyes filled with tears and throbbing of my head of how I am going to make ends meet. I sit in silence because the phone does not ring from friends to see how I am doing. I know that I can only depend on you. Everyone wants you to come tell your story, but have no money in the budget to pay you. Give a sister a gas card or something, if I have inspired you enough to call me back a second time look out for the cook out. Then the loneliness, you know how I feel Lord; I go to sleep every night alone. I have no one to tell the good things that are happening in my life or that special someone to encourage me when I am feeling low. You said in your word Lord, that you would be there for me, but you are so far away. I hate feeling this way, I do not like sleeping long hours and crying because of a heavy heart. Oh, Lord help me please help me. I know I do not need a man to live, I know my supper on my table will be sufficient, I trust that you will make a way out of no way, because you are God and God alone. The struggle is not mines it is the Lords and I wanted you to see during one of my toughest moments, that I am just like you. My radiator started steaming in the Caddy, go ahead and laugh, spending all that money in a car, well I do not have the money to buy a new one and plus it is paid for. My refrigerator has eggs and butter and every dressing a salad can handle, out dated milk and a freezer filled with frozen vegetables and a couple bags of meat. If it were not for my Sister Teka helping us out I would have to depend on a food pantry for assistance. I did not go to my church or any other agency that would have given my family help, I kept it in the immediate family and family always lends a hand when in need. I get lonely, I struggle, and I want the best for my children. It took a diagnosis to bring me closer to Him and I accept what it is for what it was to get me were I am today. I appreciate the Kyeshia Cole reality show, The Way it is on BET the theme music, Just Like You, yeah I am no different than you, and you no better than me. We all go through hardship, and tragic situations, it is how we handle the breakthrough to get through… "I love my past, I love my present. I am not ashamed of what I've had, and I'm not sad because I have it no longer." - Colette

TODAY'S SERMON

"**A**nd if it seem evil unto you to serve the Lord, choose you this day whom ye will serve; Whether the gods which your father served that were on the other side of the flood, or the gods of the Amorites, in whose land ye dwell: But as for me and my house, we will serve the Lord." Joshua 24:15

My Pastor, Bishop Beatty delivered a power message that I had to put it on paper. I took advantage of the message and applied it to me personally, finally realizing from a message from God that it was a set up. What kind of set up you may wonder? This message, sent to set me up to become a virtuous woman of God, possibly a wife. I feel the nurturing taking place and I must obey the signs. I have been disobedient to the facts that placed before me repeatedly, still me wanting to do me instead of waiting on God. The subject was "Choosy Father's Choose Jesus". He set the scenario of the old TV commercial "Choosy Mother's Choose Jiff"; you know the peanut butter commercial, yeah I see you bobbing your head. As a single mother and the head of my household, taking on the earn income credit for my children, buying clothes, shoes, food, paying the mortgage and the daily needs that applies to the day to day living for me and the girls, without CHILD SUPPORT! It was time for me to stop and evaluate my circumstances. As a mother I must pay attention to how I am leading them, (my children) because I am who they follow. When choosing a mate I must notice some qualities like Joshua. I was very humbled and receptive to the word that I praised Him with all the might I had. Any man that is wanting a relationship with me must possess these most important qualities in order to say they run it. He must be a priest and have a plan for our family. Now I must admit I am paraphrasing what I learned because as I said I applied the message to the change I want to see within my home. This special person must be a priest, the head of the household, the decision maker, the one that says we will pray together, eat together, and represent in all functions of keeping the household in order. What had my wheels churning for more was when pastor said, "When the family is united it will endure trials that come your way." This was so powerful. "If someone knocks at the door, the man of the house should be present to represent that he is leading his family." Now many of you may get off track, what if he is at work or out of town on a business trip, What if it is during dinnertime. Think about it, I know somebody did not catch on to that yet. He must have a plan for the family, "the Christian father must have a spiritual plan for his loved ones, if not the family will be doomed", my pastor says. He must possess a Godly character and must stay in constant contact with God. This man must be genuine and have an authentic character, because God is the same God yesterday, today and tomorrow. This was a set up and I thank God for using the man of God to relay this message. I was dealing with a fighting spirit that wanted me to endure loneliness and depression, to believe that no one would ever want me a woman with AIDS and it written boldly on my forehead. The devil does not want me to be happy and that booga caused me to run off that special someone because I was afraid to love him. He could have been the husband that God had sent for me. Well it was not but through him, he prepared me to get ready get ready, get ready. Now I started with the sermon now here is where the struggle tugged at me. A very special guy asked me out, we began dating, and I grew very fond of him and him of me. I was a basket case, dealing with the why me instead of why not me. Why can a man ask me out and mean it? Why must I feel all men are the same? I took him on an emotional rollercoaster and it was not fair. He said something to me that I will remember forever, "Take a look in the mirror and pray to God and ask Him to remove the spirits that are not of him. Ask him to help you to discern and for wisdom." Because the stupid stuff that I had been saying to him was not right. The next day was the sermon, "Choosy Father's, Choose Jesus" and I got my joy back, not the joy the devil stole, but the joy I gave to him. Thanks First Lady. I felt then it was time to get my house in order before unity can surface into the floral garden of sweet passionate aroma of God's will.

MIRROR

Mirror

When you look in the mirror

What do you see?

I see brown eyes, full lips, clean white teeth,

Thick eyebrows and a nose like my mother

I see the perfect forehead, surrounded by thick, black wavy

Tresses for my stylist to adore

I see a mocha colored diva, a virtuous woman of God

Look a little deeper

I even see a woman scarred.

I see my envied eyelashes that many wished they had

I even see the line of my clear contacts

Cause my eyes are bad

Look a little deeper

I see a warrior fighting for a cause.

I can wear any pair of earring, my hair all types of styles

My tongue snaps like a mousetrap

Taking control of that now

When it sings can send chills through the crowd

When in control

I'm seen not heard

Now that I've calmed down

Look in the mirror what do you see?

I see a mother, lover, friend, teacher,

preacher, sister, educator, student,

A woman independent with compassionate a seeker of

Peace I see me, Not HIV! "By His Stripes, I am healed!"

MY BLACK BROTHERS...I LOVE EM"

One day I was going through some old music and pulled out my Angie Stone CD. Thinking to myself there are some good men out there. I listened very attentively to the words of the song "Brotha". This chapter was a blog entry on my personal my space page. I wanted to put it in the book as I wrote it for my fellow readers subscribed to my blogs.

Blog Entry August 6, 2007

You may wonder where I am going with this I wonder the same thing. I have had this blog set on diary all weekend long, pondering what I am going to say to my fellow, faithful blog readers. Well for starters, do not get caught up in cyber dating on my space! Yeah I am a witness and bold enough to speak on it and I am going to share my experience. I dare not put the person on blast because as I say all the time a person will take you as far as you allow them to. I want each of you to stand your position on what your reasons are for using this resourceful service. One thing I do not do is search for a potential baby daddy, my oldest just turned fifteen on Wednesday and my soon to be thirteen year old on next Friday. I rather fly first class up in the sky than changing Huggies and wiping noses. So take this time right now, look at my profile, and tell me what you think...I am waiting...look at it. Does it say pole dancer that I am going to blow your mind and ride you until the sun comes up or does it say cover girl for a local magazine. If you chose the last one, you are correct. Sorry I do not have trophies for the correct answer only real talk, especially for those vulnerable due to lack of self-esteem and valued self-worth. Not all of the guys are like this on my space, you have your prophets, your ministers, your poets, your musicians, your authors, your fathers, your business owners, your politicians, your rappers, your radio personalities, your filmmakers, etc and you have your hustlers. Now hustlers come in different forms, I am not talking about your typical on the block, selling hot items, but hustling love. Do not take my kindness for weakness because I am a child of God first. According to my faith at this time, this is the order of my life. When I was in the world, it was kiss what I twist and worry about the risk later. Unfortunately, I was a victim to a charmer of the heart, believing the things that excited him about my beauty were true.

Why, because I already knew I was beautiful not conceited about it, just confident in my appearance. However, if you do not have control of your mind and heart you will fall prey to, I am gonna to get you sucka! Well it started three Fridays ago a very handsome tall specimen of a man contacted me through message on my space. We will call him Big Daddy. Indeed, he was, stop judging and just listen. Ohh yeah he said all of the right things and touched me in all the right places. We were practically neighbors, 10 minutes away and had much going for him, except he was not using it to his fullest potential. If you try me, I am going to write about you. As the sauce of the matter marinated in my bones, I realized I started catching feelings for Big Daddy. Yep, almost whooped, almost and there is so far away, thank you Jesus. Well we dated and let me school you brothers that take sisters out in the Queen City; we are, well I am tired of University Lake. That is the first date for most of the QC male my spacer's, me I grin and take notes. I told you I write everything, ask my friend Michelle Brooks. He told me he loved me on the first night, now I have the biggest 1000 watt light bulb shining over the entire lake instead of my head as an indicator that dude thinks I am vulnerable. Well he soon changed his game when he saw that I was not the one to play games. He then changed it to my spirit he was falling in love with and that God sent him here for me. That truly sounded nice, He quoted the Bible and everything…but even the devil knows the Bible, but he is not going to live by the word. Even though we spent time with each other, something was still a tad bit fishy about him. One day, yawl nosey, I see you all into this mess. This is the climax so get ready, go get you a swallow of Pepsi, kool aid, what ever you do before I continue. Okay you are back with your snack. I went on his page to leave a sweet comment and another woman had left a very serious one the same day. The comment conveyed that a relationship had blossomed and had grown strong and that they were still seeing one another. I am a lover of music and words and I tend to read deeper into situations sometimes more than what it is worth. What does the music have to do with it; well her page was full of love songs, specifically talking about lovemaking and together forever. This was a clear indicator of a wolf in sheep's clothing, and he was in her #1 spot. Well the sister had a comment that stated she missed him and could not wait to see him tomorrow. I had to grab my inhaler, two puffs and an Ohh hell to Da No! Not only did she want to know who I was, I wanted to know who he truly was. We corresponded and he had told her I was his sister's friend. I immediately erased photos comments, pictures and called him only to get lie after lie after lie. I spoke more than what I anticipated to tell, but I said I was going to keep it real. The moral of this story is "We don't see things as they are; we see things as we are." –Anais Nin. As my friend Mr. Keeping it Real says, "Let God counsels your relationships and marriage." Caught up in the hype of feeling relaxed that God has finally sent the one and forget all about Him. We tend to call on Him when things are going wrong, but when relationships are going right in our lives we forget about who made it possible for us to feel this way. I did not, that is why I was able to discern the wolf with the urban wear and the Air Jordan's. He was speaking the word as if he was a street minister reaching out to souls desiring closeness with God, and me the soon to be first woman by his side. Now I am not the one to come down on the sisters that bare the big derrieres with the spaghetti string thongs, but to encourage my sisters to be respectful of whom they are and cautious of the message they are sending out. I changed my profile from the gold shirt that showed a bit too much cleavage, because my forty-dollar push up bra had my puppies looking very sweet and my profile received more hits than ever before. My brothers read all of the profiles on my space; it is self-explanatory what my mission on the page. If you message me on the backend, do not expect a match made in heaven, because I am conditioned to listen to my Father more now than before. No, this incident did not make me hate men and I am not set out to bash them either, not even the one that set out to deceive me. My issue was with me mainly, and somewhat him but something I credit him for is acknowledging that I was a strong and powerful woman and when I fell into the girlhood stage of asking him, why me? He responded, "Why not you?" Looking back over the situation I got my feelings hurt, however, like everything else I bounce back. Just know you can not keep a good woman down, many responded after this blog posted and everyone said keep your head up, all I did was remind them, that with a head down I am in the position to pray. My brothers I love you and my sisters love yourselves more and remember "Life is what you make it, always has been, always will be." –Grandma Moses

I TOOK OFF MY OLD CLOTHES

My church celebrated our sixth Annual Women's Day Conference August 10-12, 2007. I did not attend any of the workshops, but on Sunday the 12 the Holy Spirit was in the house. By way of Columbia, South Carolina Pastor Jena Harold was the anointed woman of God, a prophet, a minister of the gospel, a songstress, the speaker of the hour that allowed God to use her through His mighty word, which set my soul on fire. My old clothes burnt up in the flame, which is why I took them off. Now do not let that statement sit with you too long, you might not catch up to the rest of my testimony. I must give you a vivid picture of where I was before new breathe was breath into my again defenseless body by addressing my before so that you can feel the joy I celebrated after the calming of the storm. This was only a temporary situation making room for an extraordinary thing to transpire in my life. I honestly know who my source is my Pastor Beatty taught me that in Bible Study. That God is my source for all the things I need, want and feel. If only I trust in Him and believe in what His word says. Therefore, it was not a problem when my long-term disability claims specialist called me and told me that my long-term benefits will terminate. Because of the extensive advocacy work that bombards the internet when you Google my name. Check out www.rasberrirose.org. She told me that it looked as if I could work at least on a part time capacity. Not a problem this is a blessing. Even though the devil wants me to believe that I suffer from anxiety due to emotional distress, I simply do not claim just breathe through them saying thank you Jesus, the devil is a liar. The heat and my medications do not get along so I remain in the house during the hottest hours of the summer. I stay in the igloo my friends call it hey cool air kills germs. I do not even want to elaborate no more on the wolves in sheep clothing that I met all summer long. I have to admit they were some wonderful men, whom seemed to be potential keepers and others just friends. Well to no avail, they all were just simply in the way. My God is a jealous God and He wants not only me, but also you to be so close to Him that His amour covers and your shadow protects, thanks Elder Sings. Did you get that? I honestly feel that God is preparing me for this magnificent man of God, only because I asked Him to. So now, I no longer worry about being lonely because I am never alone. Last I counted I had over one thousand my space friends, church family, my earthly family and friends but at the end of the day none of you matter if I do not have God. He is my Father, my confidant, my healer, my Savior, my friend. A severe depression cast upon my mind and tricks began to play the games I allowed it to play, all because I was weak. The pity party, the feeling of unworthiness, the disrespect towards others and slothfulness sunk in. I did not want to do anything no less go anywhere, including church. I was dealing with a spirit that I had asked God to remove from me and it came back without permission. This negative disruption tugged at me as if it wanted to stay and sometimes I felt too overwhelmed to fight. "Get away and stay away, I would say, By His stripes I am, healed and anything unlike you I rebuke in your precious name Jesus!" I wanted to sleep it away after the tears, known as the pity party. All of this and on top of that the continuous beating up on me for living a promiscuous lifestyle, searching for love in all the wrong places and ravishing my body with AIDS. Statistically I will always be defined as an African American woman with AIDS, I asked God if sex offenders can be removed from the list, why that I am healed can I be removed, "Ask in My name." He said. For you that are reading you will never know how bad this is for me, even a person that is positive we all suffer differently, for this is very emotional for me. I cannot even speak for my kids, if they come home and I am not there. My cell phone is blowing up, do not let me miss a call their minds are wondering if I am in the hospital again. I hurt when they hurt, which is probably more than I am, because I have affected them with my poor choices. I honestly did not have a reason for not attending the conference, I wanted to. I had felt like an outcast lately, I attended church and got what I needed to get out of what I went for and immediately following service I would head for the nearest exit. I would speak, smile, cry, sing, nod my head in agreement, pray and leave after receiving a well delivered word. One of my members asked me one Sunday, "Hey Sugar, you do not say much anymore, are you alright?" I simply replied, "Yes I am okay, sometime a woman needs to be seen and not heard and if you listen you can hear." On the morning of the 12th, the devil was trying to wear me down. I know it was he because my head was hurting and my stomach was aching and suddenly a gust of filtered air came across my head and swept me out of bed. I started grooming and applying makeup, getting my clothes ready for Sunday morning service. My Daddy rescued me; I thanked Him and went on my way, His way. Missionary Harris our Assistant Pastor delivered a powerful word. I would have missed that word if I had allowed the devil have his way. After service, I went out the door and down to the back of the lot where my Sedan Deville sat. My oldest daughter ran after me asking permission to go out to eat with a fellow church member. I said to her, "Fine, but I may not come back for afternoon service, so ask her for a ride home." If I had not come back, I would not have received what God intended for me. All of the women of New Covenant were to wear white or purple. If you did not have it, they insisted that we came anyway. I came back with a black and white dress on. At this time, I did not own anything white. I also did not march in with the women of New Covenant; I sat in the back row in the far left hand corner of the church. The church filled with different shades of women in various sizes, helping us celebrate the closing of the Women's Day Conference. Songs filled the air from our newly formed Youth Praise & Worship Team. The offering taken up after the reading of the scripture, then the welcome address and the beautiful women of NCBC marched in off Yolanda Adams' "Victory". Then the introduction of a woman with accolades of author, prophet, pastor, mother, wife with a pecan brown skin tone. She addressed us as seeking the broken vessel, the ones in the dark, the ones that do not want to let go of her past. That woman was I. I cannot speak for anyone else's experience, but my, my, my. My experience was a life changing one. Pastor Harold asked the women of God and all that were present to join hands and to begin having a conversation with God. "Say something to Him!" she said All I could say repeatedly was thank you Jesus! As we touched one another, a jolting sizzle went up and down my body, a feeling like no other. I was not fearful; I was ready to be free of the burden that attracted my attention. She spoke on the pity party, how she too been molested, "Call it what you want to call it, she said. Raped, violated, your innocence taken." I cried as she spoke of the broken vessel that just needed a little tuning. The woman that had my hand to the right of me and five others let go and proceeded out the door, just as the energy was just beginning to electrify the building. Ushering in His presence as we whined and wailed what it was we wanted God to know. I do not know who the lady was on my left that had my hand, but the Holy Spirit was bouncing back and forth between us, then I felt my left hand release sweat as if someone had my hand. Remember the person that had my right hand had left, or did He. Do not sleep you will miss something if you are not paying attention to how God shows up and shows out. After the Aretha Franklin, sounding voice of Pastor Harold sang her song it was time for the word. Pastor Jena Harold asked for all women who had been raped, molested, or subjected to sexual perversion of any kind to please come to the alter. I came from the back, preceded down the center aisle stood flat footed, and directly in front of the Remembrance of Me table. She spoke of the sickening wrongs that favored my childhood horrors. The vivid memory she expressed as he crept into her room in the wee hours of the night when she was a little girl. She spoke boldly about people not knowing what someone has gone thru. "You do not understand her pain, which is why she wears red lipstick and daisy dukes, show cleavage and wear clothes too tight because of the attention she long desires. She stated, I was called a jezebel, until I researched her and read up on her and realized I was not, who they said I was." She told us how God had delivered her from many things and He is still working on her through women lost. Her mission is to work with Him. (God) I am feeling enormous pressure in my chest, huffing, and puffing at the magnified memory that lodged in my head of my distant past. The past that I had forgiven and tried hard to forget what had resurfaced in an instant. At this moment, I am feeling as if I am giving birth and truly beginning to feel pregnant. About to give birth, seriously I am about to give birth my friends. I shook and shivered as if a shot of anesthesia administered to ease the pain. I cried and my nose ran like a dripping faucet. I held hands with my best friend Michelle Brooks to the left of me and on the right one of the deaconess of the church. I began to cough uncontrollably and rocked back and forth. Then I heard the pastor say, "Bring her to me." Guided towards her direction with cloudy eyes, I see nothing but a blur and her silhouette that is before me. "You are about to give birth to something my sister, something large, I reach thousands of people and together we can reach more! You have a book in you." She continued. "And I want a chapter in my book. What is your name?" "DeVondia" I say to her. "Do not let me down; I want your chapter with your name on it, DeVondia's story in my book." I flew backwards as she touched my head my ears began to burn as she cupped them with her hands. My neck started to pulsate as if my heart had moved there instead of in my chest. She touched my head and I fell. I did not pass out I just fell. My lower extremities became numb and unresponsive to the unattached feeling the upper torso needed for support. "Get her up! She yelled. Get her up! She needs to hear this even the devil can deceive… (Paraphrasing) I was assisted back up as she recited the words to a song by Aretha Franklin. She spoke of why her attitude was nasty and how no one should pass judgment if you do not know what someone has been thru. Like the clothes in my closet, everything shows cleavage, my hair and my make up to others may seem seductive, but to me it enhances my beauty. The beauty I struggled so long to recognize. "You are beautiful, like yourself, love yourself", she spoke softly. I nodded as her hands held my teary face, she began to speak in tongue and delivered a message that I will never forget, the devil is busy and before the year is out you will birth what is impregnated inside of you, beware the enemy is going to attach you my sister." Illuminate the masses is all I could think, Thanks Echo, Blackface, the Poet! I thought of you my friend as this transpired and I stood back and the tears began to dry up without the need of Kleenex. I thanked Him and remained fixated on that thought, I stood in that spot and watched others receive their deliverance, only if they wanted it. I sat down and Michelle grabbed me around my neck and said, "DeVondia did you hear her." I began to cry again with extreme tears of joy. My God sent a woman of God two hours away from Columbia, South Carolina to prophecies to me in a way that was a dedicated confirmation that the time is now. "Get ready, get ready, get ready!" She said. Receiving the information she said to me will leave me a target for attacks and how I handle them is exactly that, how I handle what the enemy was going to try to throw my way to get me off course. I went into the fellowship hall and greeted my church members, all of whom have heard my testimony and knew I had written a book. As I listened to them, say confirmation repeatedly my mind was saying, to the doubters. I knew what the

Lord had said to me and now through her. Pastor Harold spotted me from across the room with a smile. I went to her, we embraced, and I told her a brief synopsis of my diagnoses and my healing, a speaker and a soon to be published author. She winded her hand all around my face and said, "Praise God! I will get your information," she said." "No, I will go to the car and get it for you." "That would be great." she responded. Just that quick the enemy made his presence known as soon as I went outside the door.

THE DEVIL IS A LIAR

I went outside into the parking lot exiting from the fellowship hall to get a business card from my car. I myself was not hungry I did not desire the cuisine prepared for us to enjoy, mainly because my belly was full. Remember I am pregnant and ready to give birth. For those of you that are mothers and have experienced labor and delivery. During labor you do not want fried chicken, collard greens, potato salad, macaroni & cheese, rice, cornbread and banana pudding, do not forget the ice tea. You want that baby out, Ice chips and popsicles that is it! I had an issue that has long been resolved but at that time, this particular person wanted to speak on something I apologized for to the person that desired my words of forgiveness. Well when I say I was free, but they wanted to dig deeper than the old DeVondia would have allowed. Pastor Jena stated that God had delivered her from many things, however that fighting spirit was one to reckon with, the same with me. I possess a 380 with the right frame of mind to protect me and mines and a two-piece that will warrant EMS attention. So do not push me to close to the edge. Yawls remember the song. I stood as a virtuous woman and handled my business, free of the demons that shackled my feet for so long. Pastor Harold said the enemy was going to be ready to go toe to toe with me and that sucker came in the form of an individual, rather two trying to tip my boat. She continues to talk and express herself a little too much. Let me explain if I have apologized, I genuinely did just that, seriously I take that to the bank. However, as a woman walking a new walk, I submitted to obedience, but please do not continue to bump your gums as if hours ago we were not standing in front of the Remembrance of Me table together. I am free, I said. "I hear you, but do not let it happen again." She said. As she is walking, off. Now I said I am free, now keep it moving, I walk off and she keeps saying as I smile and thank Jesus for doing the right thing. My advice to anyone that needs someone to stand in for him or her as a mediator when confronting someone makes sure he/she is a pure woman or man of God. Be there for your sister or brother and let them know when they have overstepped their boundaries, because the river can be full of people swimming for help. I thank God that He has taken me from my childish ways because the devil tried to pick my mind by allowing the playback of the incident to go on and on, until I took control and pushed stop, thank you Jesus. Do not let anyone steal your joy. Even church folk or should I say so called church folk.

MY DAILY BREAD

As I come to the end, because every chapter closed comes a start of something new. I simply evaluated whom DeVondia was and made up in my mind that I wanted to trust God and do His will. I know that God will tell me first before man will tell anything about the things that will happen in my life. Through it all, I endured and made it over to the right side of the tracks, I am not perfect, but I am getting better at being me. Even though my house was broken into twice, I had to hustle fish fries to make money to make this book possible; I still have not met that knight in shining armor to sweep me off my feet and made me his wife. I am all right. I educate myself daily and thank God for all of the things that I have gone through, because at the end of the day I am simply nobody trying to tell everybody about what God did for me. I came to realized that this was a faith thing, not me thing. If you do not believe, you are dead. You know Satan wanted to take over Heaven but he could not so he decided to take over the world. I made up my mind to walk with Christ, in His spirit. By submitting myself under His ways and it is tough, Lord knows it is, humbling myself by coming out of my selfish ways to ways of the spirit, the right ways. By doing all that I can do and stand in faith, God has a hedge around you and me too, He is not going to put us in the fire by ourselves and leave us. I believe that He is not going to put no more on me than I can bear, because the same Satan that tempts us tempted Jesus and God is the same God then, today and tomorrow so the Holy Spirit will protect me even if I do fall to temptation. HIV and AIDS is a disease that is 100% preventable and it is important to stay negative. Encourage your friends and family to get an HIV test and go back for the results. Discourage negative behaviors that can put you at risk for the disease. If you are infected and you know it, seek medical care and take your medications daily, at the same time. As you can see you are probably just like me, I am no different from you, my blood is still red, and my heart still beats and I still believe what God did in my life He can do it for you. If I knew then what I know now, Lord knows things would have been different for me. There were times I felt I did not belong, many more times when I felt I was not beautiful. I could have continued to waddle in self-pity. I know many of you feel were I am coming from. Many of you are struggling/struggled with self-esteem

213

issues, not having daddy around to show you what to expect from a man and how one should be. I know some can identify with molestation as a child as I was. I learned from an episode of The Oprah Show that I was raped, not molested. I struggled with this matter for many years, honestly I told my mother about it in 2005, molested by a female and male family member at separate occasions, different houses and same town. I did not elaborate on who it was in the content of this book; however, the experience is actually my beginning. Having to break the silence was a burden worth releasing from my shoulders that felt I was suited up for a Panthers game. Please do not feel sorrow for me because as I say in my closing speeches, it could not have happened to a better person, the one that is destined to become who I am today. I went wrong for so long all for the sake to belong and to finally know who I truly am, now that I know I am beautiful inside and out I hope my words help bloom the rose that is inside of you.

DeVondia R. Roseborough

Book Club Activity

GO GET TESTED!

About the Author

DeVondia R. Roseborough is an HIV/AIDS Advocate, Author, Motivation Speaker and Founder/CEO of the Rasberrirose Foundation Inc. This Traveling Advocate provides Real Talk for Real People through her personal testimony, education and drawing needed awareness to HIV/AIDS. DeVondia enjoys working with young people and has two beautiful daughters. Look forward to upcoming books Baptized in Warm Milk based on Temptations of the Flesh and It Goes Down in Creektown.

For Speaking Engagements and Book Signings contact:

704-712-9046 or email Rasberrirose@aol.com

Proceeds from the sales of Put it on Paper will benefit the
Rasberrirose Foundation Inc.

www.Rasberrirose.org

For additional copies: www.lulu.com/devondia